push the emotional buttons that get people to buy

barry feig

AVON, MASSACHUSETTS

Published by Adams Media, an F+W Publications Company
57 Littlefield Street
Avon, MA 02322
www.adamsmedia.com

ISBN 10: 1-59337-516-6
ISBN 13: 978-1-59337-516-4

Printed in the United States of America.

J I H G F E D C B A

Library of Congress Cataloging-in-Publication Data
Feig, Barry.
Hot button marketing / Barry Feig.
p.   cm.
Includes index.
ISBN 1-59337-516-6
1. Selling—Psychological aspects. 2. Consumer behavior. 3. Consumption
(Economics)—Psychological aspects. I. Title.
HF5438.8.P75F45 2006
658.8501'9—dc22
2006014705

This publication is designed to provide accurate and authoritative information with regard
to the subject matter covered. It is sold with the understanding that the publisher is not
engaged in rendering legal, accounting, or other professional advice. If legal advice or
other expert assistance is required, the services of a competent professional person should
be sought.

—From a *Declaration of Principles* jointly adopted
by a Committee of the American Bar Association
and a Committee of Publishers and Associations

Many of the designations used by manufacturers and sellers to distinguish their product
are claimed as trademarks. Where those designations appear in this book and Adams
Media was aware of a trademark claim, the designations have been printed with initial
capital letters.

This book is available at quantity discounts for bulk purchases.
For information, please call 1-800-872-5627.

contents

THE 16 HOT BUTTONS

dedication and acknowledgments

There are many things that go into the writing of a book, both physically and psychologically. I'd like to thank Lynn for putting up with my mood swings and for helping me change my life. Joan Marie Moss who has been working with me nearly forever, for helping me to turn gibberish into something literate. My editor, Jill Alexander, whom, after I wrote 90 percent of the book said, "This is a good start." My agent, Ed Knappman, who, in a moment of weakness, decided to work with me.

I'd especially like to thank my Dad, who although he can't get around as well as he'd like to, gave me incredible insights into his mind. Gee Dad, why did it take you 82 years? And my Mother, who took time away from her pottery classes, grudgingly, to answer key questions.

I'd also like to thank all the people I've interviewed over the years who allowed me to peek into their hearts, minds, and souls.

Thanks to my new granddaughter, Megan, who inspired me to new heights, just for being there.

And thanks to the usual group of suspects. You know who you are.

introduction

To paraphrase Charles Dickens, in certain ways it is the best of times and the worst of times . . . for marketers that is. There are more products and services to sell as well as more people to sell them to. But many marketers (and I always include salespeople in that word) are faced with a problem. They're selling a physical product, but consumers are buying from the heart. Consumers buy from motivations they're not even aware of. Those motivations are the Hot Buttons of marketing, a motivation that makes a prospect's heart beat a little faster and their palms a little sweatier. Hot buttons are the keys to the psyches of your customers.

People don't buy products and services. They buy the satisfactions of unmet needs.

In my business of developing new products and positioning brands, I make a great many presentations. I sold the services I provided and occasionally made a sale. Then I had an epiphany. Why sell what I do? Why not sell what customers want to buy? I decided to sell on emotion. But which emotion? It was then I learned that every person had at least one hot button I could capitalize on. It could be the desire to look good for a boss, the desire for self-achievement, the desire for power and dominance. When I learned these hot buttons, my closing ratio went from one in twenty (optimistically), to five out of eight.

In doing my work, I conducted hundreds of interviews and interactive focus groups and found that consumers are rarely buying products, they are buying fulfillment. And from talking to these people and many others, I learned the hot buttons of marketing—and why people buy what they do.

Sixteen hot buttons may seem like an arbitrary number. However, they have been driving the human race since before the dawn of civilization. The times may have changed, but the hot buttons have remained the same. In writing this book, I asked people what their hot buttons were. Many said money and health, of course. But on further questioning, they wanted money to control things and buy things . . . maybe to impress others. Money was a means to an end—not the psychological hot button in and of itself. In fact, most people, when asked what they would do if they won the lottery, said they would give much away to their families (see Hot Button #5—the Family Values Hot Button).

The hot buttons in this book have come from countless interviews with businesses and consumers. The legwork has been done. Now you just have to use them to make the sale. The same old, same old selling techniques just don't work anymore. There are just too many people saying the same things. You need to find your customers' hot buttons and push them.

The hot buttons in this book are not in any particular order because different people have different priorities. So feel free to jump into them any way you like. I also suggest two things: Try to mentally fit at least one hot button into the product or service you're selling; and memorize them all, for they are the building blocks of consumer purchasing behavior.

Also, you don't have to be a marketer to use this book. If you just want to learn why people think the way they do, or learn how to get others excited about your thoughts and ideas, this book will give you a head start, because more than anything, this is a book on human behavior.

Barry Feig
feig@barryfeig.com

······ **the hot button principle**

you're selling what?

Way back in the olden times, before digital cameras were invented, George Eastman, the founder of Kodak, rallied his sales force around him. He asked them a simple question.

"What is this product we are selling?"

The sales force was puzzled. "Cameras," said one.

Mr. Eastman shook his head from side to side.

"Pictures?" asked another.

Eastman again said no.

"Film," said yet another.

"No, my friends," said Eastman. "You're all wrong. We're not selling any of these. Those are just the by-products. A camera is a piece of hardware that anyone can make. We're selling memories. Memories of good times. Memories of family. We are creating memories."

Kodak is still creating and selling memories after all these years. By the way, George Eastman's marketing ideas were so strong that many people think he invented the camera. He didn't. He was the pioneer of the message. Leap forward to today. To the high-tech world of microchips, video screens on cameras, and digital camcorders that record the first breath of a child—as well as a family picnic, a walk in the park, a wedding, or a little child seeing Mickey Mouse in person for the very first time. Thanks to today's wonderful high-tech miniaturizations, we can carry around a homemade movie in our shirt pocket. Instead of carrying pictures in our wallet, we're carrying picture CDs, shirt pocket DVD movies, and Web site addresses with our photos. We're also carrying cell phones embedded with cameras so we can share our pleasures instantly—before they even become memories.

We are an instant-gratification society.

But with all these high-tech advances, what are consumers buying? Memories. Recollections of family fun. Souvenirs of self-achievement. Replays of valued emotional moments. Joys of discovery.

This may be a different world from the one a century ago, but the same hot buttons that turned people on then are turning people on now. They are the hidden secrets to sales success.

what is a hot button?

Gotcha. You're reading this book. Something grabbed you and made you pick it up. Maybe you want to use the ideas to make some money for your business or family. Perhaps you were excited about learning why people buy. Maybe you thought it might be fun to read. It doesn't make a difference, but it was important to the publisher that it struck your nerve and hit at least one of your hot buttons.

A hot button is a cue that triggers an emotion in a prospective buyer. It's a cue that causes a person to buy something or to execute some action. A hot button is an emotional pull, or even a statement that makes the earth move for someone. A hot button is a turn-on for the consumer. It's how you talk about your product and speak directly to a consumer's needs in terms of his or her personal buying motivations. There are people who say that marketing, selling, and advertising are about how we *change* what others think, believe, feel, and do. But it's much more effective to work *within* a consumer's mindset.

There are two reasons people buy products and services.

1. The rational reason
2. The real reason

Humans have an incredible reservoir of rationalizations they can employ when you strike their emotional chords. People may say they buy because of rational appeals and logic. But, in the real world, consumers are neither rational nor consistent in their purchasing behavior. If they were, marketing would be easy. We would all be rich.

For proof of the power of hot buttons, look at the fascination people have with spectator sports and its related apparel. It defies reason. People don't root for a player, although the player may have some sort of transient relevance, as much as they root for a logo or a uniform. As Jerry Seinfeld said, "We're cheering for laundry!" We identify with players making $10 million or more, who have no identification with their fans, and who may be dropped or traded from one year to the next. We wear their logos because we want to identify with the team and become part of them, even if we can't realistically expect to join them. We want an association with other fans. It's a form of camaraderie (a hot button).

the hot button principle

The great fighter Rocky Marciano once said, "Hit the heart and the head will follow." It works like that in business also. Win the hearts of consumers (even—or especially—business-to-business consumers) and their minds will follow. Pushing hot buttons is how you get the buyer to say "yes" and reach for the credit card or check. The key to building relationships is to know your customer's hot buttons. This can be a company sell or a consumer pitch. Hot buttons work for services as well as products. They work for fifty-cent candy bars and $300,000 homes. No matter what you're selling, you're dealing with humans who buy more on emotion than any kind of logical thought process. A real estate broker may sell a house, not only because it's a good house but also because it has a plum tree growing in the backyard. The plum tree is part of the customer's hot button for nurturing and growth. Brokers often have the owner bake a cake when a prospective buyer is viewing the house. It makes the house seem more like a home and the aroma becomes a metaphor for family values (a hot button).

The Hot Button Principle means you stand on the same emotional footing your customer does. Instead of making your prospects change their behavior and opinions to adapt to your product, you adapt to your consumers, learn their thought processes, and find out what keeps them awake at night.

Identifying and then fulfilling a consumer's emotional need is much more effective and less expensive, in terms of money, time, and reputation, than the traditional corporate mentality of "we made it, now sell the features and the physical benefits." By establishing the hot button link that wins the hearts and minds of consumers, you make your product or service something of great emotional value. The rest of this book will show you exactly how to learn your prospects' hot buttons and incorporate them into every stage of marketing— especially selling.

some basics on needs and wants

Every marketing book will tell you that in order to create or sell a successful product you have to fulfill a consumer need. But herein lies the problem. Our basic physical needs, like food, air, and water, are satisfied quite well. But even in these basic categories you can add hot buttons to make consumers think they're getting something special. Thus, marketers pour water into an upscale-looking bottle and charge outlandish prices to make consumers think they're unique for buying a particular brand of water. By doing that, we push a hot button that will allow consumers to think that paying for water is something special—even though it's something that they used to get free! For instance, a person in a bar may order Aquafina on the rocks. It makes no difference that Aquafina is bottled from local reservoirs and that the ice is made with plain old tap water. To the consumer, the status appeal of Aquafina (or another "water of the month") makes them feel special, and a bit elitist. Does any reader out there know that Evian spelled backwards is naive? But I digress.

Since our basic physical needs are fulfilled, you need to engage your customer's wants to make a sale. Wants create new needs. It works like this:

Latent need
Stimulus (your product or pitch)
Desire (emotional buildup)
Emotional want

an iPod is not an insect

Consider the iPod, for example. The world was not waiting for the iPod, a digital music player that holds and plays back scads of songs. CD players and cassette players worked quite fine. But consumers were interested in a small device that could hold tons of music. When the iPod was introduced, most of the music was "stolen" off the Internet, so people thought this was a smart (a hot button) way to play back music. They were beating the system.

As consumer awareness of the product increased, a bandwagon effect took place. Consumers wanted the iPod and they wanted it desperately enough to pay $200 or more for it.

In short, the introduction of the iPod created a whole chain of events by identifying an emotional need and creating a want. However, this vital process started long before the iPod hit the market. The makers of the iPod invested time and money to discover various emotional hot buttons—and then made a successful product to fit. It didn't hurt that the product could be worn around a person's neck so he or she could be part of the cool elite and develop an affinity bond with others (yet another hot button). The iPod wasn't even the first mini-player. Rio was. But the Rio never touched emotions like the iPod did. Now, of course, there are many similar products on the market made by huge companies. But, none (drum roll!) is an iPod. According to a researcher who spoke to a bunch of iPod owners, many admit they never use it, but damn, they look good wearing it around their necks or pulling it out of their purse.

Discovering and fulfilling your consumer's needs reeks of Marketing 101. These principles may sound rather simplistic; however, they are often forgotten in the striving to bring a product or sale to fruition. No matter what your business is, or what you want it to be, it depends on selling something to someone else. The most efficient way to do this is to take the path of least consumer resistance—to find a hot button and push it.

one-sentence hot buttons—solutions to life's problems

If you can't sell your product in a single sentence, you really don't have an effective selling proposition, no matter how exciting or useful your product is. That's why headlines were

real-life example   A person wrote a classified ad in the automotive section of a newspaper. He was trying to sell a Jeep that had a snowplow attachment. His ad talked about the virtue of the vehicle—low mileage, new tires, great engine—typical car stuff. No response. He was only one of many trying to sell a similar vehicle.

Then he ran the following ad in the Business Opportunity section of the local shopping newspaper: "Start your own snow removal business—Late-model Jeep with plow. Be your own boss." The Jeep sold the next day. The ad played on the Control Hot Button. No longer was the buyer at the mercy of his company or boss. It was always going to snow where he lived. People were always going to need snow removed. The buyer of this new "business" was better able to stay in control of his finances and his life.

invented. Having five mediocre stories—or benefits—is not nearly as effective as having one strong banner—or benefit—that pushes a hot button.

When we relate a sales story in one sentence we are taking a shortcut that relates to a person's heart. The more time we spend on our product story (longer than one sentence) we are actually dulling the edge of our sales hook.

hidden markets, hidden drives

Our brain, and our whole body, is made up of automatic behavior patterns. These patterns help us respond to a red light by stopping, a green light by proceeding, and a yellow light by supposedly slowing down. These trigger mechanisms are so strong that they even override conscious thought.

Marketers usually see relationships between physical needs and promotional decisions more easily than they see what's really behind the sale. It's easy to see why. Marketers aren't always aware of the needs a product is made to fulfill. To make this statement stronger, marketers are *rarely* aware of the customer needs they are trying to fulfill. That's why 90 percent of new products fail, and—to extend that further—that's why 90 percent of sales pitches fail. Marketers and salespeople needn't take that as a knock, because consumers themselves can also be totally unaware of their own innate needs. They're not totally sure of what need—or want—they desire satisfied. However, consumers don't have to recognize their need or be able to articulate it. You, however, do, in order to function in the marketplace, whether you're an engineer, a salesperson, a CEO, or an R & D (research and development) person. Hybrid cars are a great example. People say they want to buy the new Toyota

Prius because it gets great mileage, or because it is good for the environment, when they're really buying it to make a statement. The cars are selling because of "reverse chic." The car, with its strange looks, says, "I care about the environment and you don't. I'm smart and socially responsible, and you're driving a gas guzzler." It's one-upmanship to the max. The appeal of the funny-looking car is so strong and laden with emotional hooks that the car is not so much sold as it is bought. It's a marketer's dream.

Consumers usually aren't aware of their needs unless you show them a stimulus; that is, they aren't aware of a need for a product unless you show them the product and how it's going to affect their lives emotionally. Consumers can't want what they don't know about. Who would want a goop of silicone in a plastic jar? But show them Mars Mud (available at Disney World and other places) and you have an instant sale. Watch how consumers mold it and play with it in their spare time—almost unconsciously. What are the physical benefits of Mars Mud— almost none. But it's fun! A successful product is more than just a sum of its product benefits. It bonds itself to the consumer by developing an emotional link that contributes to the buyer's emotional well-being. We all want to be special. Self-deception and ego gratification aren't all bad, even in this supposedly more serious century.

While a product can help consumers feel special, you can't factor the Hot Button Principle into a spreadsheet. You can't pull a hot button out of a by-the-numbers research study. Business schools almost never mention hot buttons because they can't be quantified. And it's hard to sell a hot button strategy to management because it's difficult to graph or compute.

But the Hot Button Principle is something extraordinary. It's marketing magic, especially to the bottom line. Emotional involvement is what builds loyalty. It's what makes consumers buy your product even when they have run out of coupons. As we saw in the water example, hot buttons make consumers choose your product over a parity product, even when it costs them more money—or *because* it costs them more money. Hot button marketing means adding to your product through imagery and association. It answers the two key questions that are part of almost every purchase: How is this product going to reach out and touch the consumer? and How is it going to improve the consumer's life emotionally? It's about adding a touch of salesmanship to your product through subtle cues and clues.

learn your customer's hot buttons—and achieve your goals

What we're talking about here is connecting with your audience. Connections alleviate the tenseness that comes from wracking your brain searching for the right things to say while hoping your prospective customers will respond positively. Loosen your tie; forget about wiping your brow in anticipation of getting a "no." Hot button selling is fun, because you're exploring facets of the human personality. You're not marketing against consumers. You're helping them fulfill a need.

A few years ago, marketers talked about the benefits of relationship building in creating a sale. Hot button marketing is similar—only you are learning how to further the selling and marketing process by building a relationship with your customer's *inner* self.

don't believe what consumers say they want

Learn a consumer's wants and needs for the moment and the future belongs to you. The frustrating part is that consumers don't need or want anything until you hit the right sales note. The consumer world was not frenzied with anticipation when the first bread machine was introduced. Few people said, "I wish I had a machine that baked bread." Why? Because the store-bought stuff was pretty good.

But a funny thing happened when that first bread maker was introduced. People's latent need for self-achievement (a hot button) rose to the surface. The enjoyment potential—yes, enjoyment, or fun, is an emotional need—struck a nerve. It was much more than the desire for warm bread or to save money that drove the success of the product. The bread-making process solved an innate need to create something. The end product also bombarded the senses with the aroma that wafted into the air and reinforced the self-achievement hot button.

Of course, your product has to include some kind of physical benefit and be priced within reason. But consumers choose a product more because it appeals to their self-image than because it fits into their budget. A consumer's self-image has traditionally been ill-defined. It's not how a consumer sees him or herself in reality. It's how they see themselves as they aspire to be.

the myth of parity products

One of the marketing person's most difficult jobs is building market share for a so-called parity product—one that has no apparent advantage over existing products. Why do some products magically succeed in building and maintaining share dominance while others face the prospects of playing follow-the-leader throughout their life? Successful products offer consumers a positive emotional benefit. To make the consumer want your product more than once, you have to make the consumer feel good about buying your product every time. Terms such as "parity product" and "low-interest products" are really self-fulfilling prophecies probably coined by marketing people who don't realize that every consumer product has its own emotional footprint.

the key to unlocking impulse sales

Hot button marketing is the key to impulse sales. In an impulse product the whole rationality of the purchase decision is short-circuited. The consumer has no time to think, only react. You, as a marketer or salesperson, have to do everything you can to spur that reaction. For example, many consumers start their day with a workout at the local gym. They get up at 5:30 A.M. to sweat and toil. They ride stationary bikes and climb StairMasters that go nowhere. But at the end of the workout they might spy a local dessert shop and order the pie of the day ("no whipped cream, I'm dieting"). They explain it away by saying, "I've earned it. It's a reward for a job well done." That may be the rational reason, but the purchasing decision was the result of impulses.

marketing insight

In a no-emotion, logical world, lowest prices would win hands down. Indeed generics would corner almost every product category. But this isn't an emotionless society. The spoils go to the marketer who best makes consumers feel good about themselves.

Can you indulge yourself without actually eating or drinking? You can if you watch a good commercial. Did you ever watch a beer commercial and see all those good-looking people downing beer after beer and having the time of their lives. They're so happy and smiling. You see the beer being ordered, poured, served, and drunk and you almost feel satiated. Hate to disappoint you, but you really didn't see them taste the beer. Your taste buds may have tasted the virtual beer but the actors didn't taste anything. People never actually drink anything in beer commercials. It's against some kind of federal law to actually drink alcohol—even fake alcohol—on a TV commercial. Whether they drank it or not is not really the point. You would swear they drank it. Your brain filled the gap and you took part in a virtual drinking experience. It captured your hot button for a stimulating experience—almost drinking the beer was fun.

You picked up on the commercial's visceral and emotional cues. You even heard the sound of the beer being poured into the glass. These auditory cues brought an emotional halo to the product. The smile after the actors almost drank the beer caused you to think it was a good-tasting and satisfying product. If the beer was drunk in a friendly convivial atmosphere, you saw yourself as being with friends (a hot button). The happy, satisfied face was the payoff of the commercial. You indulged yourself—without even being there. The auditory and visual cues brought the product to life, almost like that cold can was really in your hand.

hot buttons and business-to-business selling

Many people are afraid to use emotion in business selling. They're afraid to approach companies like IBM, Xerox, or American Express or other corporate heavy hitters because they are gigantic conglomerates and might dismiss such an approach. Remember the old saying about speaking at meetings and pretending that the audience is wearing underwear. It works the same way in business. You're not selling to a corporation. You're selling to a *person* in a corporation who may have the same hopes, dreams, and hot buttons as you do. Even when you're selling to the CEO, you're selling to a person with a family who may want status, approval (two hot buttons), and recognition from stockholders. You can undress him by finding what makes him tick—his hot buttons. The president is no different from the mailroom clerk, who wants his boss to tell him he's doing a good job. Of course, you'll have to figure out how to find the president's hot buttons before the meeting, but you'll learn how to do that in the following chapters.

analyzing needs—and avoiding the hard sell

There is much confusion in the marketplace about consumer needs, especially on the technical side. Mostly the confusion lies in what benefits to apply to goods and services. Promotional messages for consumer needs often have strong technical tones, which potential consumers don't understand. Users don't know how to distinguish one product from another or how to select from the different choices even when the technical terms are brought down to their levels. Articles, literature, and talks about new products and services have often advocated the importance of "satisfying end-user needs," but writers and speakers tend to look at things from the "this is what makes us special" angle, and fill their communications with talk about technologies, techniques, and standards. This leads to the hard sell—grasping at straws and parroting the features and how hard it was for R & D to put the pieces together and make the product they are so proud of. Perhaps they believe that this is the best way to convey messages of excellence. But it leaves the customer cold.

Hot buttons negate the need for the hard sell or grasping at straws to make a sale. Consumers don't care about how hard your product was to make. Consumers only care about themselves.

End users do not need to know about the electronics inside these machines, how they function, or how to activate and check them from time to time. The trick is to find out why people are buying the machines. The tech-head might want all the bells and whistles, because he or she wants the best and most-equipped product. This same tech-head may want the newest digital camcorder, loaded with features he or she might never use—but with great showoff value. The teenaged digital camera "social buyer" might want a minimum of technology—just enough to take quick pictures of her friends and good times. Another teen might choose the camera that looks the coolest. It all comes down to different hot buttons.

marketing insight

The whole Budweiser empire was built on a mission statement that had nothing to do with making beer. One of the founders of Budweiser, Adolphus Busch, summed up his mission statement—a hot button idea (no, it wasn't called a hot button at the time) summarized in two sentences. "Our business is not just making beer. Making friends is our business." The tiny sentence "Making friends is our business" was the hot button impetus that quickly set Anheuser-Busch apart from the competition. The desire to belong (see Hot Button #6) is a strong hot button.

nice-to-have vs. want-to-have

There are two phrases that are necessary to learn when using the Hot Button Principle. They represent different degrees of needs.

- *Nice*-to-Have
- *Want*-to-Have

It's up to the product and you, the marketer or salesperson, to turn the former into the latter. For example, customers usually say they want to buy from a socially conscious company, but that rarely translates into sales. Most of the time, if you ask people about disposable products and packaging, they'll say, "I won't buy a product that pollutes the environment." However, more often than not a nonpolluting product offers a Nice-to-Have benefit but it is not a dealmaker, especially when the product moves into the Want-to-Have category. In the Want-to-Have category, rationalizations go into high gear.

what are wants?

Do you know what the number one pollutant found in landfills is? Newspaper. That's right, in spite of the major recycling

---

real-life example   Campbell's Soup Company ran a series of focus groups for its new microwave soups. At the beginning of the discussion, people swore that they would not buy a product that polluted the environment.

"No way," they said, almost in unison. Then they were shown the product, a microwave soup, clad in a foam container. They wanted the product dearly. "This will pollute the environment," they were clearly told. Did this statement, that went counter to their expressed beliefs, change their mind? No.

They said it was a quick way to get a hot meal for their kids and themselves. It solved the time bind (a hot button) they considered themselves facing. A pollution-free container would have been "Nice-to-Have." Microwaveable Campbell's Soup in a cup that kids could prepare themselves or that Mom could prepare in minutes was a Want-to-Have. It struck a hot button. The end benefit was more important than polluting the environment.

drives. And the ink used in most newspapers is not biodegradable. It is poisonous and can sometimes leach into the water supply. But even though newspapers are a major source of waste and there are many alternatives available, such as TV, radio, and the Internet, newspapers are a *want* because they are our number one source of gaining knowledge (a hot button).

You must keep grilling consumers on their purchase preferences. People once thought it would be fun to connect to America Online. Then they became addicted to it. They didn't realize how important AOL had become to them until the system broke down for a few hours. AOL had become a "Must-Have." Must-Have products usually provide an emphasis on satisfying a hot button. Only when you combine product reinforcement with satisfying a hot button can you create anything approaching total brand satisfaction and a Must-Have product. But once you've melded the two, is your marketing work done? No! The market is always shifting. Even as you are reading this chapter, products are evolving. America Online has more competition than ever before as new companies push the Desire to Belong Hot Button and the Family Values Hot Button.

heartfelt segmentation

Consumers are always on the lookout for new products and brands. Thus, new selling pitches based on shifting hot buttons and Must-Haves need to be developed. Despite the advances in marketing techniques, most market segments are dominated by the idea of selling the most products for the fewest dollars without any regard for the consumers' hot buttons. They fail, despite Rocky Marciano's rule to go for what matters most— the heart.

Go for the heart. Make your product story pithy and terse. Remember that brand imagery and the products and services we choose indicate our contentiousness and status, or our friendliness and loving nature. Hot button marketing cuts across all geographic areas. Ultimately, marketers must determine and understand the real drivers of sales, provide an understanding of how a brand or product can be relevant to these drivers, and include all of these at the heart of every sales and marketing plan.

Heartfelt segmentation can be considered a new kind of segmentation. In heartfelt segmentation you uncover and push the buttons of a group's shared emotional values. The old segmentation strategies based upon identifying large, homogeneous groups of consumers that share some basic physical or demographic characteristics such as age or income is not as effective today as heartfelt segmentation. Our lifestyles are changing; people pick and choose from a mixture of brand possibilities as they construct their own unique identities. This phenomenon means that you have to change your way of selling, and the media you use, to communicate your message.

A person cannot explain how they *experience* a brand nor can they always articulate how they *feel* about a brand. Hot button marketing addresses this issue by accepting that an underlying aspect of individuals and the behavior they exhibit is composed of primal instincts, drives, needs, and motivations. The way to a consumer's pocket is through the heart. And that is the soul of the Hot Button Principle.

The warrior crouched just west of the entrance portal. He was a great hero, a defender of a godforsaken place, a champion to his people. He had taken lessons in stealth from the warriors that came before him. However, he loved the thrill of the kill. Stealth was not his style. He was a warrior, pure and simple. So the warrior engaged in a frontal attack that, while brave, elicited fatal fire from the returning armies. He was utterly defeated in combat.

Is this a scene from the Macedonian wars? No, it is a scene from a paintball contest. Paintball is a game, where fun-loving, competitive teens and adults shoot each other with globs of paint. People travel hours and hours to find a paintball park, which other people built for just that purpose. As silly as this sounds to a nonplayer, paintball, which has millions of participants nationally and internationally, is one of the twentieth-century ways of achieving power and dominance, one of the key hot buttons. Paintball is the modern form of the joust, only a lot messier.

As a marketer, what hot button would you use to get people involved in paintball? You might stress the Power and Dominance Hot Button (see Hot Button #15). You might stress the Fun Hot Button (see Hot Button #7)—or even the Desire to Belong Hot Button (see Hot Button #6). Whatever hot button you leverage, it's been done before. Hot buttons are universal—and timeless. Lean on these hot buttons, because in sales and marketing you (ultimately) don't get points for creativity. You get points for selling. That's what's reflected in your paycheck and your balance sheet. Hot buttons are the building blocks of sales, much as the alphabet is a building block to words, stories, and essays.

how universal are hot buttons?

American Indians have used objects called *fetishes*—hand-carved images of animals—for more than a thousand years. A fetish is a symbolic carrier of a message—a touchstone that represents the individual's search for satisfaction and satiation. Native Americans carved symbols of the animal whose attributes they aspired to possess. The badger represented aggressiveness and industriousness, while the mountain lion was associated with resourcefulness and leadership. The Native Americans drew power and strength from the fetish by placing the nostrils of the fetish to their mouth and taking deep breaths—presumably to inhale the essence of the characteristics it embodied. We don't use fetishes much anymore. But we do use products and services. We play games like paintball, or patronize an upscale coffee chain, in order to display the characteristics we envision for ourselves.

The power of hot buttons slices through geographical boundaries, cultures, and eras. China, before its surge into manufacturing, was one of the most egalitarian of countries. People traveled on bicycles, not in cars. Yet, they bought counterfeit labels of the most prestigious bicycle manufacturer. Why? They wanted to show off their new "top of the line" bike much as we in the United States like to show off our Mercedes— or Prius. In the United States, people are spending to acquire "genuine" fake Louis Vuitton luggage and the like. Different countries. Different products. Same motivations.

american indians? paintball? masai warriors?

So, why is the universality of hot buttons important to you? Because, in the next ten years, experts conservatively estimate that 35 percent of the United States will be made up of people that are currently referred to as minorities. Now, add these cultures to the major class distinctions in the United States, and you can see the need to find a common ground. That common ground is hot buttons. How you discover and push them is what makes the difference. New

marketing insight

Consumers use products to achieve the characteristics they envision for themselves. We can even go back to Adam and Eve and the not-so-friendly serpent for our hot button search. When the serpent asked Eve to pick an apple, she objected. Then, the serpent introduced the hot buttons of knowledge (see Hot Button #14) and power (see Hot Button #15). He painted pictures of all that she would acquire by eating the forbidden fruit. "It's good to be God," she might have thought. That's the first known case of caveat emptor—let the buyer beware. It's also the first known case of a "salesperson" pushing a hot button to persuade someone to do something.

immigrants are arriving every day. Most of them, just like you, will strive to move up in class and status. Your ability to use the I'm Better Than You Hot Button will be critical. But here's the rub. The symbols of a status upgrade for one person or ethnic group may be entirely different for someone else.

In all countries, wealth is a symbol of status. It doesn't matter whether that wealth is measured in dollars, the number of cows you have, the real estate you own, the car you drive, or the brand of wine and liquor you consume. The hot buttons stay the same but the hot button *symbols* depend on age, ethnicity, and background. That's why you constantly have to re-spin your pitch and essentially reinvent yourself for each sale.

symbols—the dialects of hot buttons

We all react to symbols. Whether our reactions are external or internal doesn't really matter. What does matter is that reactions to symbols are learned. We associate the symbols with experiences and emotions that are tied to our particular culture and environment. Thus, when we encounter a symbol it evokes specific reactions. We use brands, too, as symbols to

---

real-life example   Every culture has the same hot buttons. How marketers use them depends on the culture.

Can a common fly be a symbol of status? Yes, when the right combination of appeals come together. When I was on a photo safari in Africa, I asked the guide, "Do the many different tribes have a common hot button?" He thought for a moment. "Yes," he replied. "The desire for status. The Masai people, for example, take great pride in the size of their herd of cattle. The more cattle, the higher a person's status and the more important he is in the community." The women tend the herd. The herd draws flies and the flies gather around the Masai wives' heads. No flies, no cattle, no status. Raid bug killer is not a hot product around the Masai.

express the emotions we feel when we use them. Our internal reaction to a symbol may be emotional or unemotional. Brands are initially unemotional marks (or shorthand) that advertisers use in advertising to try to tie their products into our needs. When a symbol elicits a cognitive or emotional response in us, we in turn can use it to express that idea or emotion to others.

Marketers use symbols as unspoken statements that identify themselves with consumers. Using the symbols that are common to a consumer's culture and experience says, "I understand. You can trust me."

wants, needs, and hot button marketing

While the value systems of a particular people may be different, the hot buttons remain the same. For instance, if you are dealing with a Japanese businessperson, he or she will do a complete analysis of your business card and the physical and emotional trappings of the way you do business. The Japanese businessperson values self-esteem above all else and expects the seller's professional trappings to reflect the same kind of self-esteem and confidence. In Eastern and Pacific Bloc countries, prospects will strive to form a bond with you by inviting you to their homes or to a neutral restaurant for dinner so they can learn about you and your respect for their traditions and customs. But is that so different from what we do here? Golf, sports, restaurants, and other venues where business is *not* discussed grease the way to the sale.

Hot button marketers use hot buttons to have fun with their clients. They know that sales can be fun when the parties are not considered adversaries and when they have mutual interest and goals. A friend of mine feigns exasperation when a particular

Yellow Pages salesperson comes to call. It seems like a Yellow Pages sale would be a cut-and-dried appeal for the businessperson to invest in a substantial advertising contract. Not so. When this representative calls, she asks about my friend's kids. She knows how many children he has and what awards they've won. My friend, who happens to be a very successful car dealer (who also uses hot buttons), admits that he will talk to her for as long as she wants because she knows what hot buttons to push to get him to talk. Does he really think that whether or not his new baby slept through the night is of interest to her? Of course not. But it is something that interests *him*. Now my friend may not always buy ad space from her, but he will give her pitch strong consideration. Why? Because she hit on his hot button—family values.

identifying what we really want

Universal motivations and desires are symbols that are hot-branded into our psyches. They work in tandem with our emotions. They shape who we are and what roles we play. The ancients called them *elemental spirits*. We call them *invisible links* to a person's inner drive.

Emotions are a source of power because they are one of the few elements in our lives that we can't change. We can sublimate them or try to ignore them, but they affect the way we experience the world. We filter all our experiences into and through our emotional hot buttons.

Hot button marketers know that their prospects are at the mercy of their emotions. For instance, a person who sells souvenirs knows he or she must sell the souvenir at the moment of peak emotion or the souvenir will not be sold. A boot shop owner out West knows that when a person leaves the vacation spot, he or she will forget how great the boots looked in the shop mirror. When the person boards the plane, the peak emotion will be lost, as will the sale. Other, more important, matters will enter the person's psyche.

Most of us have little control over our emotions. Emotions play a powerful roll in helping us achieve our perceived wants. Marketers and salespeople are conduits that enable people to achieve those wants. It's not uncommon in the case of an expensive purchase for customers to savor the act of writing the check for the item they've longed for . . . even dotting the eye on the check reinforces this joy. Emotions, in every culture, need to be kneaded, stretched, salved, and pushed to achieve maximum strength.

marketing insight

Consumer can't change their emotions, so you have to vary your pitches according to what *satisfies* these emotions, which will vary from culture to culture and demographic to demographic.

the building blocks of hot buttons: needs, interests, values

Just as we talked about the differences between needs and wants, there is a difference between needs and interests. Needs are non-negotiable. You want them now. No ifs, ands, or buts. Needs are who we are or what we aspire to be. They are fundamental and necessary to all human satisfaction.

Interests, on the other hand, are road maps that form our needs. Interests are like kicking the tire on a car—a form of curiosity. But an interest in something can drive a need to learn more. Learning and the desire to obtain knowledge about a subject is a hot button. That's why museums, libraries, and new

"Discovery Centers" geared to kids (and their parents) are so important.

Values are fundamental beliefs that are also non-negotiable. Values are the ideas, habits, customs, and beliefs that are a characteristic of a particular social community. Values determine how we understand the world and how we respond to it. Find a person's values and you are on your way to discovering his or her hot buttons.

America is tiled with ethnic groups. The hot buttons you choose vary with different cultures even within the United States. MCI, the erstwhile long-distance carrier, had an outbound telephone sales center populated with Hispanics calling other Hispanics. In this case, even though the bottom line was about saving money on long-distance rates, the message was 100 percent family oriented—a value that is particularly important in the Hispanic community. "Look how close you can stay to your family by phone with our incredibly low rates." The low rates were an interest. The pitch was the Family Values Hot Button (see Hot Button #5).

It's not a one-size-fits-all business world anymore. You have to custom-tailor your hot button pitch to your particular customers. It's key that you learn your customer's values and interests and cater to their hot buttons. For example, Wells Fargo is going after the Hispanic market with fervor—even going as far as differentiating the markets into various Latino subethnic groups (for example, Puerto Rican and Mexican). Wells Fargo makes their branches an intrinsic part of the sale—for instance, decorating the Mexican-oriented branches with Mexican tile—to satisfy the Desire to Belong Hot Button (see Hot Button #6) and affiliation with their culture.

generational and class influences

First-generation immigrants have the same hot buttons as everybody else, but they stay close to the values and symbols with which they grew up. They have not yet entered into a social contract with the New World. They often stick closely to traditions from the "old country" and their heritage and values. I spoke to a Hispanic representative of a bank about using translators to make a sale. A poll of his customers showed that they would think the translators were just trying to make money for the bank. Instead, he suggested that the people bring in their own translators—a move that turned out to be very successful. Another marketer who sells Hispanic food products said he won't change his product packaging for the U.S. market. He has found that it's important to keep the same look because his customers want things the way they were in the old country.

While their hot buttons remain the same, there are definite symbols that people of different so-called classes use as mnemonics. Analogies that are lost on certain working-class people can be meaningful to those who are more financially affluent. Metaphorical expressions and symbols may have totally different meanings to the various classes.

real-life example   Banks are moving into the "family" business big time. Bank of America recently developed a product geared to the Mexican Hispanic market called SafeSend, a new money-transfer product. Now, instead of chasing the train after a long week of work to hand-deliver money, a Mexican National can grab a phone and punch buttons to transfer, say, $700 from her checking account to her SafeSend account. Bank of America zips the money to a special account that can be accessed by 20,000 ATMs across Mexico. Back home, the recipient carries a SafeSend card that Bank of America sends to the family home via a next-day courier service.

For example, consider advertising, which is a sales pitch in print. Different people see and hear the messages in a variety of ways. Eastern Europe provides an interesting case study. Television played a key role in the democracy movement there. In one case a resident in a newly democratized country saw a house cat eating from a silver bowl on TV. He assumed that all cats in the West must eat out of silver bowls. Thus, he assumed that humans must definitely have better lives in a democratic society.

In an actual example, a car salesperson lost a sales opportunity when he showed a college student from a working-class

real-life example   The Starbucks people have gentrification down to a science. One of their recent plans had a goal of opening 1,500 new stores around the globe. But what are they selling? Most people would say they're selling expensive coffee. But that's not what drives sales. Starbucks is selling community and companionship, as well as prestige. Starbucks is adept at manipulating its customers' emotional vulnerabilities. By and large, Starbucks' clientele are not day laborers but people who strive to seem upscale. People (even if they don't realize it) show their class by holding the well-known Starbucks cup in their hands as status symbols. A cup of Starbucks acts as a beacon that they are wealthy and smart enough to pay extra for coffee.

Unlike many other coffee and fast-food shops that focus on selling more products per customer through heavy promotions like "dollar" menus, "value" meals, and "get one free" punch cards, Starbucks never cuts prices. Starbucks marketers know that their customers consider the Starbucks cup with its brown corrugated "holder" an affordable luxury that has virtually no substitute. You can hold a business meeting, or even a first date, over a Café Grande. You can't do that at McDonald's. Starbucks has obviously learned that hot buttons are the same around the world or they never would have made the commitment to become a global fixture as well as an American phenomenon. For the middle class and its aspirants, consumer habits, like a regular visit to Starbucks, help build identities that satisfy a hot button yearning that is in our psychological self-interest.

background a used luxury car with all the prestigious trimmings. The car was "just not her," she said. "It would make me feel too uppity around my friends." She settled for a lesser Toyota even though the price was the same, because it was much more like the cars her friends drove. For her, the desire to belong was stronger than the desire for prestige. The salesperson's approach probably would have resulted in a sale if she had been an upscale Ivy Leaguer or wealthy coed who had grown up with prestigious goods and learned to appreciate all the symbols of success.

People who are lower on the social ladder often prefer tangible goods rather than services that have only abstract benefits. Their hot buttons are often about being smarter and getting the most that one can get for the money. They achieve prestige and success though tangible displays of power, rather than through the intangible symbols that services provide. For instance, while a wealthy consumer might employ a live-in maid for status, the maid might show off her new prestigiously named designer handbag or brag about the new, expensive sneakers she bought for her son.

hot buttons in advertising

Think times are hard? A 1958 *Life* magazine claimed that there were months when the owners of advertising agencies had to live with the frightening thought that a right guess about how to sell a product might make them a fortune while a bad guess might make them shine shoes for a living. That same article pointed to something new in the ad world that was going to take the guesswork out of advertising—motivational research. They wanted to learn about hot buttons—even though they weren't referred to as such then. At that time, the major advertising agencies made copywriters get out of their offices and interview real live consumers. From these interviews sprang such classics as the Marlboro Man and the Swanson line of TV dinners, which promoted "good-for-your-family nutrition"—not speed.

In the case of the Marlboro Man, interviews showed that the brand, introduced in the twenties, had a feminine image, as did filter cigarettes in general. The research showed that men wanted a rough and rugged, manlier image. The agency researched a wide variety of "masculine" settings, the strongest of which proved to be the cowboy performing manly tasks that men could aspire to, if not actually participate in. The TV dinner came to fruition because Swanson had an excess of turkey. Consumers rebelled when the product was positioned for convenience. They felt like they were letting their family down—they wanted real nutrition along with convenience. When marketers changed their pitch, the TV dinners became a hit.

In the same time period, prepackaged cake mixes were ready for prime time—but buyers weren't ready for cakes you could make by just adding water and baking. Consumers thought it made them look like they weren't doing enough for their family or were just plain lazy. A motivational researcher thought about that dilemma. He came up with a radical idea. "We're doing too much for the consumer," he reasoned. "Let's take the egg out of the mix and have consumers beat in their own." It was a marvelous play to the consumer's heart and was responsible for all the cake mixes we see today.

Today, of course, consumers buy a great many products that just require them to add water. Many are already premixed batters that the consumer just takes out of the refrigerator and bakes—but then consumers have evolved to the point where they see these products as smart rather than a sign of laziness. Poverty of money has lost to poverty of time. Women actually feel good that they have products that allow them time to please their families. They feel smart for buying the premade cakes and batters and welcome the time these products give them to bond with their families.

emerging markets and trends

Consumer behavior is a continuum. Hot buttons are being fulfilled in different ways. Global and regional consumer segments such as mature consumers and ecologically concerned consumers are finding new ways to be heard. At the same time, ethnic and nationalist identities are resulting in greater market fragmentation. There is no single culture and there are different patterns of consumer behavior. They vary with the situation and the consumer.

As consumers are being segmented, they have a greater urge to be more cosmopolitan, rather than more insular, in their thinking. Newly developing nations are developing a more sophisticated breed of consumers. Even though smart hot button marketers use different symbols—since there is no single cosmopolitan culture—they continue to focus on identifying the universal hot buttons.

chapter 3 ······

selling to the inner self

This chapter is about why people buy what they buy and do what they do. Consider it a practical foray into the world of consumer behavior. You can use hot buttons to create a strategic selling model by learning what your consumers want and fulfilling those desires. When you learn what motivates a particular market segment, you can create the images, pictures, or words that make buyers want your product. New products and new ways of doing things are big news to consumers. Hot button marketing is a blatant sell to the self. Hot button selling is about selling to your consumer's aspirations. It's about selling to the way consumers want to be, rather than the way they are.

Business as usual just doesn't work anymore. Or maybe it does, but it takes too long in this "I need results now" era. Hot button marketing is a way of thinking—not about yourself—but about your customer.

a humble rodent spawns a high-tech revolution

What has a button, a tail, costs about $10, and spurred a billion-dollar industry, the likes of which has turned the world, as we know it, upside down? Hint: Chances are you use it to kill an alien, write a business plan, or send a note to a friend.

The $10 dynamo is the humble mouse that you use every day on your computer. Computers had been around for many years, but were mainly used by hobbyists and businesses. Yet, do you think your Aunt Ethel would have taken time to master a keyboard and learn the ins and outs of computing by pressing a series of unrelated keys? No way. It was the mouse that made "point and click" a part of American language. The mouse and the Internet put the Make Me Smarter Hot Button (see Hot Button #14) into Aunt Ethel's home. It also brought the Family Values Hot Button (see Hot Button #5) into play, because Aunt Ethel was able to send e-mails and talk by computer to anyone she wanted, anytime she wanted.

The mouse was a solution to a problem—how to get people who were totally computer illiterate to feel comfortable enough to use it to keep in touch with family and friends, for entertainment, and to gain knowledge—hot buttons all. Solutions and benefits are what make people buy what they buy, and the mouse was the enabler. As a hot button marketer, you are an enabler—selling products and services that enable consumers to be what they aspire to be.

So a computer is just a computer—right? Wrong. Steve Jobs, CEO of Apple, may be the most masterful marketer of all—

maybe even more so than Bill Gates, CEO of Microsoft. Microsoft used strong-arm tactics to get Windows installed on most computers. Microsoft also used a strong graphic approach that made point and click understandable to nontechs. But Jobs used quirky designs that brought new customers who wanted something different and were willing to pay for it. A bitter war is being staged. A schism has developed between Mac owners and PC owners. Mac owners are proud of their beautiful machines and the beautiful design statements they make. PC owners don't brag about their PCs anymore; it has become a utility item. Macintosh owners consider themselves special, apart from the crowd of PC owners. Give Jobs the credit for instilling the Discovery Hot Button and the Desire to Get the Best That Can Be Got Hot Buttons into his products.

imagery elicits emotions, emotions create sales

Pictures, imagery, and words are the keys to getting into the consumer's heart. What could be more persuasive to young mothers than the words "Vaseline Nursery Jelly"? With the heritage of the Vaseline name, these three words answer all of the young mother's needs. The baby scent reinforces the positioning that this product is somehow something special. It's the Nurturing Hot Button (see Hot Button #12) that gets to a mom's core emotion.

A hot button is the visible and invisible force behind a sale. It's the sum total of the prospect's life experiences to that point in time when you are actually selling the product. As mentioned in the previous chapter, hot buttons are a product of the consumer's values, needs, sentiments, and even their cultural identity. Used correctly, hot buttons give a consumer the power to fly—in even the most mundane sales category. Even the dullest of product can be marketed "to the heart."

Let's take this example of selling a humble, "mundane" sawhorse. For those who are mechanically challenged, a sawhorse is sort of a three- or four-legged pedestal for holding wood steady so you can make useful things out of it.

Customer: "I'm looking for a sawhorse but yours are too expensive. My wife would have a fit. Maybe I should run down to Wal*Mart. Or maybe I shouldn't tell her what it costs."

Salesperson: "Before you do that, did you see the new sawhorse line we just got in? What's the color scheme of your basement?"

Customer: "Yellow, why?"

Salesperson: "We have it in yellow—your wife is going to love how it fits the color scheme of your basement. It's light, plastic, and folds, so she can move it out of the way for her step workouts. You can even show her how to use it herself to build a set of shelves for the bedroom. It's so good-looking it doesn't even have to be hidden away in a garage."

Let's see what's going on here. Sawhorses are usually bought by men. Originally, they came in basic "manly colors" like black or brown. Now the husband is buying a yellow one to both please and empower his mate. It fits the color scheme of the home, and it's made light and easy so she can use it and be proud of it. She can even build her self-esteem by making shelves to enhance her space. But there may be an invisible force at work here. Initially the buyer indicated a sawhorse didn't fit into the household budget and he may have even been chastised if he bought it. But now it becomes a gift for his wife as well as a tool he really wants. The salesman helped the man rationalize the purchase. The prospect gave the game away when he said it didn't fit into the household budget. It means that he wanted it and she didn't. However, the salesperson hit two hot buttons. Let's look at the dynamics:

1. The man had a desire to create something.
2. He wanted to please his mate with something as romantic as a piece of hardware.
3. He wanted a bit more control over his finances.

The salesperson and the product solved each of these by pushing the right hot buttons.

While this example may sound far-fetched, it really isn't. The microwave oven was originally marketed to women. The product was dying a slow, torturous death. Women were not ready for a technology that they thought might be dangerous. Besides, women didn't want to get out of the kitchen fast. It made them feel lazy and as if they were not nurturing their families (see Hot Button #12). Men liked the hi-tech gizmo, though. They did buy them—at a slow pace. Before long, Mom found that the microwave was just right for reheating leftovers and defrosting meats. Mom glowed. She could fulfill her supermom role more efficiently. No, the microwave oven was not a product that was replacing her or the conventional oven that she had grown to love. It actually enhanced her cooking experience.

hot buttons drive movies, too

Movie critic Roger Ebert was once asked what the most important factor was in voting for the Best Picture Oscar Award. His response: "The heartstrings." Ebert went on to say that a movie that touches our emotions has the best chance of success. Most movies nowadays are well researched in focus groups to make sure that people cry at the right times, laugh at the right times, and even jump out of their seats at the right times in the case of a horror movie. Endings are tested to make sure the moviegoer leaves the theater on a high note—wanting more.

The best advertising, of course, is through word of mouth. People love to discover that new sleeper movie that everyone loves. The movie *Fatal Attraction* was a huge hit some years back. It was a story about a man who had a one-time affair that turned into a disaster. The woman was totally crazy and threatened to wreck his home life, his home, and his wife. The movie was about love and hate. Men and women watched it for different reasons. The men watched because the one-night stand, that was so prominent in the movie, gave them a vicarious thrill. The women enjoyed it because the man and the woman who started the whole sordid mess got their comeuppance.

real-life example   Price is a poor predictor of sales. Very few products sell on price alone. Ninety percent of new products fail, no matter what the price. Why? Because marketers are selling through the intellect, while consumers are buying from the heart—they buy when a product or service strikes a nerve. Dan Wieden, founder of Wieden & Kennedy, one of the most creative advertising agencies and the agency for Nike Shoes, said that as long as his heart beats faster after seeing a commercial, he knows they have a winner. Price has never been a strong selling point with Nike. Pushing their customers' hot buttons is. Price is part of the Control Hot Button in that it relates to a customer's control of their finances. But Nike appeals to the Desire to Belong Hot Button (see Hot Button #6) and the Get the Best That Can Be Got Hot Button (see Hot Button #9). Are you sure of what you're selling? You might be selling something tangible, but the consumer is buying intangibles.

The movie was shot with two different endings—one for the United States and one for Europe. In the European version, the woman who started the affair lived. In the U.S version, the woman died an ultraviolent death at the hands of the wife. In Europe, where there is a more open awareness and permissiveness about extramarital affairs, there was greater acceptance of the alternative ending. Europeans wanted stimulation while Americans wanted satisfaction for their Family Values Hot Button (see Hot Button #5).

positioning can be more important than the product

A hot button made a blockbuster bestseller out of First Brand's Glad-Lock Storage Bags. Talk about marketing problems. First Brands Snap Lock bags had made a disappointing showing in test markets. First Brands wanted to know what to do. They determined that the low market share was due to poor positioning of the product, a nonmemorable name, and a product difference that was perceived by consumers as meaningless and expensive—until the Control Hot Button (see Hot Button #1) came into play.

First, a new bag was developed with a seal that changed colors when it was closed. Focus groups were formed and interviewed. Women consumers roundly knocked the product. But one woman said, "I wish I could get my husband and kids to seal the bag and keep foods fresh."

The Glad-Lock people altered the "sell" in the next round of focus groups. They changed the basic positioning of the product to allow the consumer to "rationalize" the added Glad-Lock expense. The new positioning—"The bag that's so simple, husbands and kids get it right every time"—struck an immediate chord with women. They were excited about being able to see when the bag was closed properly and that their clumsy husbands and on-the-go kids could see it, too. First Brands then changed the name Snap Lock to Glad-Lock to reflect its heritage. All of this came from consumer input.

The new product/positioning combination made marketing history.

are you selling something different from what the customer is buying?

While customers may express a physical, logical reason for buying a product, oftentimes it is not the real reason they actually buy it. For instance, while people may choose a new toothpaste because they say they want healthier teeth, focus groups have pointed out that at least half of America chooses a toothpaste because they like the taste or want a refreshing way to start the day. It's important to understand what consumers are buying, even if they don't know themselves. On the following page are some examples of products and services together with the logical reason for buying (used by most salespeople) and the hot button reasons that buyers buy.

pushing hot buttons breeds loyalty

Many customer satisfaction studies have concluded that there is a significant relationship between customer satisfaction and loyalty. Recent studies have shown that emotional hot buttons are a core attribute in satisfaction and result in positive word of mouth. Positive word of mouth has the highest correlation with customer satisfaction and is the highest predictor of a product's

product/service	logical	hot button
Vacation trip	Have fun in the sun	Fun; learning about other people; something to talk and brag about; sexuality; discovery
Fashion accessories	Functional value	Get the best that can be got; affinity with social groups and classes
Prepared soup	Fast; nutritious	Family values; nurturing; control over a loved-one's health
Cosmetics	To look good; cover a scar or blemish	Become a new you; be the best you can be; sexuality
Underwear	Basic need	Sexuality; control; protection
Candy	Good taste	Stimulation; fun; romance
Doctor's visit	Treat an illness	Control over health
Vitamins	Supplement diet	Be the best you can be
Diamond ring	Express love; adornment	Control of loved one; sexuality; get the best that can be got; prestige

or salesperson's success. Contrary to popular opinion, the opposite of love is not hate—it's indifference. And marketing works the same way. Going for the middle ground is difficult, because when you try to appeal to everyone, you appeal to few.

people eat differently when they're alone (or the dynamics of situational marketing)

Hot Buttons are dynamic. They depend on the prospect's life stage; that is, what stage a person is in his or her life. Obvious things to look at include age, family situation, job status, psychological profile, and other factors. But, many researchers look at those physical attributes and neglect to look at a person's psychological makeup. "When I was divorced," said one woman in a focus group about self-awareness, "I went on a binge of knowledge-gain and self-improvement." But when she was interviewed further, she admitted, "I didn't want anyone to know I was alone." Her desire to belong was stifled, so she expressed herself through different hot buttons.

Some time back, Gerber introduced a line of foods called Gerber Singles. Gerber either forgot or chose not to remember that their brand was associated with baby food. More importantly, they also forgot that people didn't want to be hit in the face with the fact that they were single. The positioning was a disaster. Neither men nor women wanted to advertise to the world that they were alone by carting a week's worth of the product up to the checkout line.

According to focus groups, women tend to be more self-conscious about being alone than men—but a compendium of men and women agreed that it's more fun doing something with someone rather than doing it alone. One woman said, "I don't want to be seen by myself because it looks like no one cares about me." But men, when interviewed in focus groups, have expressed the same concerns. "When I went to the wedding alone I felt odd. It looked like everyone was having a good time with their partners."

People are social animals and demand that someone make them feel special, if not to themselves, then to someone else. This changes as people move on to different life stages. Being a bachelor may be okay when a person is in his twenties, but by the time the same person reaches his thirties, he may feel that he should be starting a family and that there is something wrong with him if he hasn't found someone. He may even be stigmatized by his paired-up peers. Hot button marketing takes into account what life stage the person is in.

hot button products turn consumers on in a number of ways

Consumers often buy products not because of their attributes per se but rather because of the ultimate satisfaction of values that these attributes provide. A person without a lot of money may buy a cubic zirconia for his loved one, even though he really wants a diamond. It's the symbol that counts—which is the ultimate value. But value in purchases is multidimensional. Buyers actually experience the joy and satisfaction of buying in more than just one way.

- The prepurchase experience: This involves information gathering, planning, or even imagining the experience.
- The purchase experience: This involves choice, the actual turning over of the product to the buyer, packaging, the purchase encounter, and the selling environment.
- The core consumption experience: This is how the product or service actually satiates the hot button.
- The remembered experience: Remembrances of how the product satiated the hot button. This is the one that's responsible for repeat sales. As the great entertainers say, leave the customers wanting more.

Hot Buttons are also based on a person's self-concept and serve to reinforce and fulfill that concept. Self-concept often translates into a person's lifestyle, or the way that person lives his or her life. Some people may be materialistic, wearing flashy clothes and driving expensive cars, while others may instead prefer a simpler life with fewer visible status symbols. Individuals will often try to enhance their self-concepts, and it may be possible to spin pitches and create marketing to help achieve this goal. A successful corporate lawyer may respond to nurturing products and fundraising appeals because he wants to be a member of a care-giving community.

basic understandings

Hot Buttons may be obvious, unseen, and multiple. Some Hot Buttons are publicly expressed (for example, the desire to buy an Internet-filtering program to control what their kids are seeing), while others (the desire to gain prestige by buying a show piece of jewelry, for example) are not. Hot Buttons can be based on both internal and external factors; that is, a person may want a fancy pen either because he or she likes it (internal motivation) or because this will give her status among the artistic elite (external).

Hot Buttons can be based on situational behavior. Consumers with little extra time may take the first product in a store or buy from the first salesperson they see. Consumers shopping for a special occasion (e.g., a wedding) may buy different products. Consumers may buy totally different products while they are on vacation than what they would buy at home.

In conclusion, how we decide if a brand, product, or service is for us depends on how we perceive it and how it empowers us. This, in turn, depends on the frame of reference that we overlay on it. The frame of reference comes largely from our experience. Just as consumers have a mental list of brands that they associate with a given product category, so too do they have a mental list of attributes that they associate to a given brand. In most cases, marketers can only play up a limited number of a product's physical attributes. Thus, by shifting the focus from tangible to emotional attributes you can change consumer perceptions of a product. When all physical factors are equal you can use hot buttons to tip the scales in favor of your brands, product, or service.

chapter 4 ······

"Yogiisms" are quotes of Yogi Berra, who, besides being a baseball player, was also famous for fracturing the English language in provocative, interesting ways. One of his quotes gives the secret to market research and identifying Hot Buttons:

"You can observe a lot by watching."

He didn't say the following but probably would have if given the chance:

"You can hear a lot by listening."

"You can get a lot of answers by asking questions."

The essence of good research is to ask questions and listen. Listening is a lost art. Many marketing people would rather talk about their own product than listen to what others say about it. Or, in big companies, research is buried under reams of paper, so the important part—their customer's hot buttons—is never read. One product manager at a major consumer products company, when asked if he actually spoke to consumers, replied, "No, that's what my researchers do." When the researchers were asked if they actually spoke to consumers, they said, "No, that's what our research suppliers are supposed to do." No one at the company actually spoke or listened to the people who they hoped would buy their product! No attention was paid to their customer's hot buttons. The products that succeeded did so on pure luck. Yogi would probably shake his head in frustration.

seek and you will enter the human heart and mind

Learning and memorizing the various Hot Buttons in this book is only half your task (and only half effective) if you are a marketer or salesperson. You need to know how to *find* your customer's Hot Buttons before you develop your product, service, or make a sales pitch. How can you find out what your customer's hot buttons are? As we said earlier, watch, listen, and observe. This chapter presents formal and informal ways to find your customers' hot buttons. Remember, a sale may consist of pushing several hot buttons—even for the most unlikely and mundane of products and services.

For instance, there are lots of reasons for hiring a house-cleaning service.

People who start a housecleaning service think, "I'm going to do the best job for the best price." Hold it. Two things are wrong here. *Everybody* who makes a pitch to a prospect says they're going to do the best job. Why then should the prospect choose you over anyone else? Doing a good job is a given.

"Because I charge less," you might say. The problem is people don't shop on price alone. People also buy relationships.

Your prospect might have a special occasion coming up. Maybe she doesn't have time to do the cleaning herself (see Hot Button #8—Poverty of Time) and wants it done quickly. Perhaps the customer wants to impress people by having a cleaning crew wearing maid's uniforms (see Hot Button #2—I'm Better Than You). Perhaps the husband is hiring a cleaning service to say to his wife, "You're working too hard, and I care" (see Hot Button #11—Sex, Love, and Romance). Maybe the prospective client wants control of what seems like an overwhelming task (see Hot Button #1—Control). It might be because she doesn't feel good and wants to treat herself to something special (see Hot Button #12—Nurturing).

Why would a person *not* want to hire your cleaning service? You need to know that, too. Here are some negatives you might have to dodge: security, speed of delivery, fear of a stranger getting too close (cleaning people know a *lot* about the people whose houses they clean). You need to know what it is you're offering and all the limitations. Talk about the limitations in a positive way—"All my employees come from referrals and are thoroughly screened and bonded." The key is not in presenting a laundry list of benefits. That may be what you want to sell, but it's not what the buyer wants to buy. In the course of conversation you might casually mention one benefit—and ask if this is important to your prospect. Lead them into talking about what their expectations are and ask (often from past experience and feedback) what would likely play a part in the buying decision. Talk about only those issues. If you start raising all the pros and cons—most of which the buyer hasn't even considered—you'll muddy the waters and may even talk yourself out of the sale. You need to know what it is you're offering and all the limitations or threatening aspects of your business in order to address them at the right time.

research is the art of making the unseen, seen

It takes research to find out your prospect's hot buttons. That research doesn't have to be expensive. But it will take time. Well-planned research will tell you everything you need to know about your buyers' hot buttons and will dramatically increase your odds of success. But misguided research will do the opposite. It will channel your energies into the wrong markets with the wrong message. You might want to think of every call or visit, whether it's an inbound call to you or an outbound call from you, as a chance to research your customer.

Who has the magic black box for uncovering marketing hot buttons or consumer motivations? The simple answer is no one does—except you. Hot button research seeks to thoroughly understand the unspoken motives and beliefs held by customers and prospects in regard to a brand, product, or service. You just have to find it.

Recently a woman asked me to help her market a new keyboard cover. Her friends and family thought the product was a great idea. The approach made sense. She surmised that people don't like to touch keyboards used by other people because they fear picking up germs and illnesses. Even the former head of the most prestigious advertising agency in the world suggested she pursue it. However, she had to invest $10,000 for her first factory run. She was investing a great deal of money on a hope and a prayer.

She asked me what to do. I replied that she should test the product and do her research *before* she spent her money. So she went to Office Depot, where she was kindly allowed to test her product in the store. What she found was amazing.

"Barry," she said, "Nobody wanted my product."

"Then," I said, "I just saved you $10,000. Let's try it in other markets."

She went to call centers, doctors' offices, insurance companies, and other places where people share computers. It turned out that she was solving a problem no one cared seriously enough about. She never found the right Hot Button because there was none strong enough. Thankfully, she didn't mortgage her house on a wing and a prayer.

the power to observe

Here's where we go wrong: We think we know why customers want what they do.

But, customers don't know, so how can we? You're going to need some tools to find your customers' hot buttons. Then, you're going to proactively control every part of the situation, because you have the power.

The first of these tools is the Power to Observe. When you interview a customer, you begin by reading his or her body language. Every good hot button marketer can read body language—like a good poker player can. When talking with others, watch their body language when you're engaging in small talk. Make it a habit to "read" people—watch how they dress, what makes them smile, what makes them start looking across the room (e.g., boredom, other interests, etc.), and what kinds of clothes they wear.

In a store or showroom situation, hide and watch. Pay attention to what draws the attention of buyers. Where do they slow down? What are they looking at, touching, picking up? Do they stop to read posters, price tags, etc? What's their hair like? What kinds of jewelry, watches, etc., are they wearing?

If they're highly motivated by ethnic beliefs, for example, their clothes and jewelry will probably be ethnic. For example, a hot button marketer who notices his prospect is not wearing jewelry might infer that the customer is not a candidate for the prestige sell. Then, when you feel confident they're ready to talk and you have gathered a few clues about them, you might ask if they're shopping for themselves or if they are buying for someone else—a birthday perhaps?

One hot button marketer considers a tour of a client's parking lot and office a key part of research. If the client has his or her own parking space complete with a painted "reserved" sign, he can infer that prestige is important to the client. He

marketing insight   Observing your prospects' office décor is a good way to uncover their hot buttons. Granted, an office tour is not usually on the list of selected research methods—but it works. Is the office crammed with pictures of the prospect's family or is there a picture of a sailboat in a prominent place? What other kind of pictures does she have on her walls—is she an adventure fanatic or is she more family oriented? Are there cute little stuffed animals and toys? What about books? What are the predominant colors in the office? These all can provide clues for salespeople looking for an appropriate hot button to push, or at least what to talk about. If the person has an incredibly neat office, he may be a candidate for the Control Hot Button. If the office is a mess, it may be the Poverty of Time Hot Button. Where you see all sorts of accoutrements that speak of sports and adventure, you might push the Discovery Hot Button. And, definitely look for evidence that the Family Values Hot Button is key to the client.

can further judge what kind of person the client is by the type of car he or she drives. A person who drives a Subaru Outback is going to need a different selling approach than one who drives a Lexus.

the power to ask questions

Ninety percent of a sales pitch should be about the marketer asking questions. Ask questions in the right way and you'll get the answers you want. Of course, some people might not open up immediately, but most will. People love to talk about themselves and what interests them.

Asking questions also builds relationships. The more questions a prospect answers, the more likely he or she will open up and provide even more information. They will also trust you more than your competitor—because you show that you care about them. Just remember, you'll never get the right answers if you don't know the right questions. The best questions to ask anyone are "why?" and "so what?" These are the questions that encourage others to explain themselves or to expound enough so that you can be sure you understand what they're saying.

Listen to the prospect's voice inflections for a look into his or her soul. For example, here are some of the questions I ask in a focus group or in one-on-one inquiries. You can use them, too.

- What kind of similar products do you buy?
- How often do you buy these kinds of products/services?
- Where do you get your information when you're thinking about buying?
- Whom would you buy this product for? Why?
- Where will the product be used?

- Would this product replace something else you already use or own?
- How often would you use it?
- How will it fit into your current lifestyle?
- How unique is this product?
- What don't you like or understand about this product?

In a business presentation, try to add:

- What about your job keeps you awake at night?

Notice that these are all open-ended questions. I call them *probes*. The prospect has to react and can't quickly respond with a yes or no answer. More importantly, every reaction is a clue to the person's inner self. And notice, too, that you haven't tried to sell anyone anything!

Obviously these are not all the questions you need to ask to successfully market your product. But if your customer responds to these questions, you will find additional answers will come more easily. "More is Better." The more data you compile and apply to each question, the better.

Feel free to write down the previous questions. Consumers won't mind. In fact, many will be impressed that you care that much.

However, don't take their comments at face value. Play devil's advocate—keep drawing out more information by challenging and repeating answers (even going back and rewording answers previously given) to clarify. Remember, anyone can talk. But not everyone has the time, patience, and discipline to listen.

the power to listen

Listening is a lost art. You can't talk and listen at the same time. It's a physical impossibility. Without questioning and listening, you have no basis for knowing what hot button will trigger a buying decision for your customer. This goes for marketers in megalithic companies, too.

Please, don't delegate your research solely to researchers. Go out and interview consumers to find out for yourself what makes your customers tick. My favorite approach is to show people fake ads or fake products—or even a competitor's product—and ask them what they think.

While you're listening you'll want to serve as a sort of mirror to the people you're listening to. You want them to see themselves in you. Repeat back to them what they tell you so they can hear and affirm what's being said. This shows that you really are listening to what they are saying. Your attention needs to be focused entirely on the buyer.

how to practice

Salespeople (and marketers are salespeople above all else) are taught to sell, sell, sell. So they sell, sell, sell. What they accomplish is making people flat-out disgusted and angry. What's missing? Backward communication. No salesperson should ever insist what's right for a buyer, until he or she solicits feedback by asking prospects what they are looking for and what's important to them. No salesperson knows so much about anyone that he or she can second-guess a prospect's needs, wants, and interests.

But since you are a hot button marketer, go a step further and take the path of least resistance. Don't "sell" what you're attempting to sell. Let people buy. Here's a game you can play in sales training and brainstorming sessions: Your task is to sell a product. "That's easy," you might say. But here's the kicker. You have to sell a product without making a statement. Huh?

Let's say you're trying to sell a washing machine:

> *You:* "What are you looking for in a washing machine?"
> *Prospect:* "One that has a big tub."
> *You:* "How big a tub should it be?"
> *Prospect:* "It should at least hold a blanket."
> *You:* "Would you consider one that would hold two blankets?"
> *Prospect:* "Yes."
> *You:* "Why?"
> *Prospect:* "So I could do two things at one time." (Hot Button #8—Poverty of Time)
> *You:* "Which machine would you like?"
> *Prospect:* "I only buy from Sears."
> *You:* "What if this machine came from the same company that makes Kenmore appliances?" (Kenmore is a Sears brand.)
> *Prospect:* "It would depend on the warranty."
> *You:* "What if I were to give you the same warranty as Sears does, and—because Kenmores are so well made—I threw in an extra year for only $59. Would you buy now?"
> *Prospect:* "Yes."
> *You:* "Where should I have it delivered?"

Or, here's an interesting twist:

> *Prospect:* "I'd like one that conserves water."
> *You:* "Why do you want one that conserves water?"

Prospect: "Because I want to keep my water bill down. I do a lot of washing." (Hot Button #1—Control)

You: "What if I had a machine that did twice as many clothes and used the same amount of water? Would you be interested?"

Prospect: "I'd like a machine that has dials for different kinds of clothes."

You: "Why? Don't all machines have that?" (You know the answer to that one but you want to keep the prospect talking.)

Prospect: "No, I haven't seen that before."

You: "How important is that to you?"

Prospect: "I don't want some clothes to be dried as much."

You: "So, suppose I had a washing machine that saved water, and I sold you a dryer with even more settings? Would you be interested?"

Prospect: "Yes."

You: "How much were you looking to spend?"

Prospect: "Under $1,000."

You: "What if I were to have a washing machine–dryer combo and sold both of them to you for less than $900?"

Prospect: "For both?"

You: "Would you like to look at the machine? Would you like to read the specs and see how much water you can save?"

Prospect: "I don't know."

You: "Why?"

Prospect: "It sounds too good to be true."

You: "Suppose it was a major brand, and I threw in the manufacturer's guarantee, and for only $79.95, I'll guarantee it an extra year?"

Prospect: "Is this reconditioned?"

You: "Why—is this important?"

Prospect: "Because it may break down."

You: "Am I hearing you correctly? If I were to give you a brand-new Maytag washer, with the dryer, with the guarantee, and with the extra warranty—you'd be willing to buy it now?"

Prospect: "For how much?"

You: "What was the price we just agreed on?"

Prospect: "Under $1,000."

You: "When do you want it delivered?"

Prospect: "ASAP."

See, no pressure. You learned the customer's hot buttons and closed the deal without a hard sell—with actually no sell at all.

people, people everywhere—find the ones who have similar hot buttons

Go where your customers hang out. Every town has networking groups. If you're selling a wine, go to bars. If you're selling sporting apparel, go to a gym. Try to set up an informal gathering of people and talk to them. You might not sell anything at the groups but you'll get to talk to people and find out what hot buttons turn them on. Social groups are fluid—people are a part of several groups that they move between. They may be only semiactive in some or all of the social groups to which they belong. They may attend meetings or participate in activities only rarely, depending on what the group's immediate activity is or depending on which of the groups is the most interesting or demanding at the time. The more you can understand that the easier it will be to understand the consumer.

Finding those people can be as simple as having coffee after church (many offer coffee socials after services) or, for that matter, attending any social event. Talk with people about any-thing—*except* the sale—and try to find out what makes them tick. They might react to Ms. Molly's hat, and you can find out what or why they make the observations they do. It might not be anything you use specifically in a sales situation with them, but you'll start to put two and two together—to see relation-ships and patterns that you'll use in your sales either to those individuals or to others.

A segment of consumers may look the same on the surface. But that's not the reality. Each individual possesses character-istics that you need to understand to ensure the best contact strategy. Learn what triggers their buying responses. You can connect with your audience when your communications are relevant, convenient, and deliver real value for recipients.

don't try to be all things to all people

The key to developing a successful marketing program is to make the earth move for a specific someone. Heartfelt Segmen-tation—appealing to the heart and the hot buttons—are the rules of the day. There are only two Heartfelt Segmentation Strategies. Both work.

1. Find people who need what you make and sell it to them the way they want it sold to them.
2. Change your product's appeal to certain groups. For instance, you might develop three types of products— a basic performer, one with a longer warranty, and a third with all the bells and whistles you can jam in. It's called a good, better, best strategy—which might target people in several hot button segments.

Know your customers. The primary mission of segmentation is to satisfy a specific group of customers who all have something in common. You position yourself as the specialist at something—preferably something directly related to the product or service you're selling. The trick is to find your leadership position and appeal to a consolidated audience.

The major mistakes marketers make in selling are having nothing of value to offer customers and selling it badly. As every entrepreneur learns quickly enough, coming up with an idea is simple. Even producing the product is a snap—compared with selling it. Effective marketing requires understanding human nature, finding out what people want and need, and creatively offering that to the right people—and allowing them to buy.

Underlying this concept is the ability to get people involved completely and totally. Engage their emotions and involve as many of the five senses as you possibly can. Even though food never looks as good as it does in the package, showing a mouth-watering "serving suggestion" provides a fantasy of a delightful end benefit. Consumers can taste the product with their minds.

more formal approaches for finding your prospect's hot buttons

While asking candid questions about your consumer is a strong informal strategy, there are many other methods used by successful companies. All of these have withstood the test of time and all have the goal of eliciting the true motivations of consumers. No, you don't need all of the following methodologies to answer critical questions, but many can be used in a well thought out project. But nothing will happen unless you take the initiative.

putting your concepts in context

The high-strategy way to do market research on new products is to match your test products as closely as possible to what you will deliver to consumers in the real world. For instance, if a company develops a product through focus groups and uses imagery and packaging to create a message, that's what should be presented to consumers in the real world. Consumers don't buy a product in controlled circumstances. They buy a product because something about it turns them on at a given moment. It could be the name, the product taste, the company that manufactures it, or a clever copy line. That's why research in context is so powerful.

one-on-one stimulus response strategy

In this kind of approach, you interview consumers and show concepts, products, or other ideas to jump-start the consumer's mind. Research facilities are often available in malls, where the staff can set up the interviews for you. Interviews should run no longer than five or ten minutes.

telephone strategy

The telephone can provide a general overview of the market. It can be particularly helpful for the marketer on a budget or one who wants a broad overview of a market. Dig numbers out of your customer database, mailing lists, or lead-generating lists. It's hard, though, to gauge hot buttons from a telephone study.

faux ad/concept testing

Here's a research method that can be done via interactive groups, one-on-one interviews, the mail, or touch screens. Consumers react to concepts that are rendered into hypothetical, or "faux," ads. Consumers react to all the parts of the ad as well as the entire concept. You define the buttons from whatever element gets the consumer excited.

forced-choice assessment

This is another research method that can be done in focus groups, in one-on-one interviews, and even in telephone studies. Ask respondents to choose from similar products. The marketer makes conclusions on possible hot buttons based on the pattern of responses.

interactive consumer groups

Commonly called *focus groups*, interactive consumer groups are among the most used of research tools. A focus group is a selected group of people with similar purchasing habits or demographics gathered in a conference room to discuss your product. They are the most helpful research tool—and the most misused. The trick to using focus groups is to have consumers respond to something. It can be a package, a name, or a concept in context. Don't ask consumers to intellectualize about a product—you're interested in their first reaction. People don't intellectualize in a store—they either buy the product or not.

long-form questionnaires

If you are doing a questionnaire, use more response-generating essay questions rather than the typical "how do you rate the product questions" and yes/no questions. It's hard to put this data into computers and challenging to analyze, but it brings much more useful information. Make sure you're getting the reactions you're paying for. Your future success depends on it.

the business-to-business link

When you have a business product, talk to businesspeople in your industry. Most entrepreneurs don't believe ostensibly busy people will give up their time, gratis. They're wrong. Businesspeople are the easiest people to approach. If they know you're not trying to sell them something, they're usually thrilled to spend an hour or more talking about your product and the hot buttons that turn them on. People love to give advice and promote themselves as experts.

the five-minute guide to learning your consumer's hot buttons

Hot button research doesn't have to be the slow, tedious process most companies use. It should be exciting and vibrant as you search for new ways to develop business opportunities and new strategies to open up the consumer's skeptical heart.

do it quickly and efficiently

Create an inventory of hypothetical product positionings. Allow your mind to relax and keep a notepad with you. You can even set up a brainstorming session with others you know. The strongest ideas—a judgment call at first—should be developed into actual full-color ads. These will serve as the backbone of your hot button research plan. Pretty quick, wasn't it? You can get local college art students to do artwork inexpensively if you don't have a willing advertising agency or art department.

Take these out to a local mall—preferably one that has a consumer research facility. Have the staff buttonhole consumers and show them the concepts. Never allow respondents to read the concepts—a great many people are embarrassed over their reading ability and many won't be able to comprehend the message. Instead, read them aloud as you show your concepts. Watch for your respondent's reactions. The main purpose of the mall intercepts is to identify red flags about your concepts so you can change them.

Once you've made your changes, take your ads out to interactive groups (focus groups) in whatever market you're selling. Ask consumers which concepts turn them on. Ask about each aspect of the ad. You're not going to ask consumers what they want. You're going to show them. You're going to make your respondents react to your concepts. Each group should be a microcosm of the shopping experience. When they get excited, it shows you struck a nerve—a hot button.

After these groups, lick your wounds and modify your concepts again. Throw out the bombs. Modify the ones that received lukewarm interest. Add new concepts based entirely on the reactions from the first group.

Then show your new collection to new groups of consumers in a different area of the country (wherever you hope to sell your product).

revise the inventory

Show the revised concepts again. If your concepts were good, you'll have a winner. Guaranteed. Here's how the whole workflow process for a typical (and almost always successful) new product works.

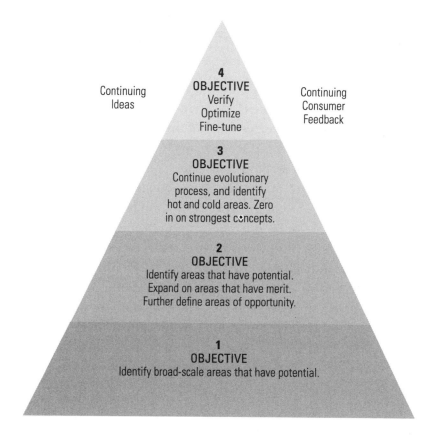

In short, there are many research tools at your disposal. Some are formal, and some are informal. These tools can be expensive, moderate in cost, or even free, but none of them are more expensive than a failed sales pitch or product that doesn't bond with consumers.

chapter 5

the desire for control

what marketers need to know

Control is one of the strongest hot buttons. It's also the one that's easiest to adapt to any product category. Control is reassurance, a virtual, implied, or written insurance policy that the product or service is going to make the consumer's life better and less subject to the vagaries of fortune. Many people think their lives are out of control—subject to the whims of their boss, the stock market, the lottery, and whether or not the person they had a date with on Saturday night will call them back. Loss of control is synonymous with a fear of the unknown. People equate loss of control with loss of power over one's own destiny—or of the destiny of one's loved ones. They fear they'll become victims. Many people think their lives are out of control. It's up to the hot button marketer to show them how they can keep at least one aspect of their lives under control.

how marketers can apply this

Hot button marketers know that change is exciting when we initiate it—and threatening when it's done to us. So they give their buyers the space they need to get comfortable with the idea of change. The success of change and innovation depends on how well the product conforms to consumers' mindsets and how well the purchase enables consumers to feel in control of their own destiny. Hot button marketers focus on building relationships of trust with their customers. And, they constantly look for ways to reassure consumers—throughout the sales process—that the decision to buy is exactly right for them—and that the price is right.

control is a good thing

Contrary to popular belief, being a control freak is not a negative thing. We are all control freaks. We all want to master our environment. You might say that the first manifestation of control was when cave people learned to build fires to control their warmth, or back even earlier when they first moved into caves to control their habitats from the devastations and chicanery of Nature. Although this is the twenty-first century and we've moved out of caves, the old control issues still exist, along with some new ones, such as:

- Finances
- Our own safety and health
- The safety and health of our loved ones
- Continuing enjoyment of our mates, community, and friends
- Our acquisitions
- What people think of our purchases or acquisitions
- Our jobs
- Our self-respect and the respect of others

Wouldn't it be great to control all of the above? As a marketer, you can create products and sales pitches that make customers feel like they can take control of their lives. Entire businesses, like insurance companies, manufacturers of baby products, beauty aid companies, online dating services, and vitamin companies, owe their success to the hot buttons of control. Chances are, you can fit your product into one of the control hot buttons.

hot button marketers sell security

You can hardly walk out of a Best Buy without purchasing insurance on the product you've selected—no matter how inexpensive—these days. Target, Kmart, and Wal*Mart are also taking up the practice of selling insurance on products they sell, even on alarm clocks and toaster ovens.

(Just to digress a bit, an alarm clock or a clock radio is control in action. It assures us that we will wake up at the right time.) Control is what prompts airplane pilots to give out information on flight delays, weather conditions, and where you are in the sky. They want you to feel in control even if you're not.

the real and unreal world of control

Think of control this way. When we want to satisfy a need, we create a picture in our minds of what it would look and feel like to have that need or desire met. (For example, if we have a desire for more money, we may visualize ourselves in a mansion or having the freedom to quit a boring job.) Control is the way we expect things to be. It's the way we want it to be.

Those who market medical services usually presume that a person visits a doctor or clinic for a specific medical condition. Research has shown otherwise. More often people are seeking satisfaction of their psychological needs—to take control over their own health. Whether a course of therapy works or not, consumers are often dissatisfied when they're treated mechanically. Their psychological needs were not acknowledged. Too many doctors are simply not reassuring their patients—or playing to their patients' Control Hot Button. That's why Doc-in-a-Box Treatment Centers—storefront medical operations, with doctors and nurses that treat simple ailments, like cold symptoms, minor burns, bruises, and cuts—have sprung up. No hassle with doctors or lengthy appointment dates. People just come in and get fixed.

Mini–medical clinics are another hot new way to get health care for minor ailments. Look for them at your local discount store in the very near future. They're actually in a few Target stores right now. The control of health—or preventative medicine—is evidenced by the millions of people who take vitamins and herbs every morning to ward off illness. It's become the modern-day version of old-time medicine men.

marketing insight   Sell the insurance policy when you sell your goods and services. Take cellular phones, for example. Cellular phones are one of the hottest products. A cellular phone gives users unparalleled access to control—control over their families as well as control for their family. For example, many teens got their first cell phone with the following rationale: "When I'm driving home from college I may have a breakdown on a dark highway." That's a prime, motivating force for parents. Of course, nobody predicted that a control thing would become a nation-wide trend. Which brought up a whole new issue. How do parents keep their kid's cell phone bills down? Answer: Providers are now issuing new phones with parental controls—a control product that controls a control product. Good grief! And a masterful usage of the Control Hot Button. They are also developing phones with a directional finder that lets parents know exactly where their kids are. I'm not sure kids are going to love that.

Yet another new way of controlling medical expenses—one especially popular with doctors starting new practices—is an idea borrowed from the online line services: an "all-you-can-eat platter." The doctor charges a yearly fee, say $750, and the client gets unlimited office visits and consultations.

The entire issue of our need to control our health and well-being can be morbid. No consumer, particularly baby boomers, likes to think of themselves as old or infirm. For this reason, insurance companies, in particular, are striving to lighten up their messages.

There is an old truism that insurance is a risky business. When consumers invest in life insurance, they're betting that they're going to die, while the insurance company is betting that they're going to live—you hope they win. This little irony is a good demonstration of how hard we try to control everything about our lives, even our deaths.

we don't welcome change unless we want it

The instinct to control our environment is resistance to change. Our brains simply are not wired for change. Biologically, our bodies are programmed for stasis. Change can be stressful. Most people are vested in the status quo. People attempt to do things the way they've always done them. They resist radicalization of their thinking.

That's why new and so-called breakthrough products and innovations usually fail. Inventors and research and development departments may love them, but such products are the riskiest ventures of all. Consumers tend to be wary of radical new ideas. They have to figure out how the breakthrough new product fits into their lives—whether it's really worth it in terms of changing the way they do things. Some people are actually scared of making the changes necessary to try a new product.

That's why most successful new products and sales pitches are adaptations of something that already exists. When the original TV dinners were developed, they were adaptations of the kinds of meals people usually prepared from scratch, such as fried chicken and meat loaf. As people started going out to dinner more, the dinners began to resemble entrées of restaurant favorites. No, they don't taste nearly as good as restaurant dinners, but people had a picture of the restaurant food in their heads. They were in control of their dining.

More than one product or selling premise has failed because its time had not come. People didn't feel that they were in control of the new technology. It took years to get people to trust ATM machines—people felt like they were entrusting their money to a soulless machine and were losing control.

In the business-to-business world, businesspeople can be outwardly and inwardly scared of bringing in a new vender

real-life example   There's an ad that depicts two men sitting on a park bench feeding some nearby ducks. One man is telling the other how lucky he was to have had supplemental insurance when he was injured and had to miss work. The second man asks what supplemental insurance is. A duck tries several times to help out, replying, "AFLAC!" The men continue talking but never quite come up with the name. The duck keeps trying to help but they're not listening. Finally the duck kicks a bread crumb back at the men. The ad was a risky approach to a very serious topic. And there was apparently some concern about whether the company, which sells cancer insurance, would use the ad. Well, they did, and the results were spectacular. According to reports, AFLAC sales have risen 55 percent since the duck ads began.

because they fear they may not have the same control as they did over their old vender. Hot button marketers assure business customers that they will be in complete control, and thus look good to their managers. In your presentations, assure your clients that you are working for their promotion.

marketing insight

Most people resist change, even if it might be for the better. Show how your product minimizes the risk. Almost all the ads for home businesses show how you can make a change for the better without risking your lifestyle. Build on it.

Nextel recently had a commercial out called "Dance Party." It depicts three tech guys dancing up a storm in the office. The boss walks in, all in a panic because he can't get some critical information about an employee and inventory. Within three seconds flat, the guys deliver the answers using Nextel's technology, and they go right back to their dancing. Now that's the kind of control that would make any boss happy.

waiting time is a key element of control

The longer people wait for something, the less control they have (or perceive they have) over it. It's not only the instant gratification of seeing pictures in seconds that made the digital camera so popular. People were able to correct exposure mistakes in seconds, unlike waiting for days for the film to come back and finding out the photo shows that dear old Aunt Alice has a tree growing out of her head,

Car dealers insist on deposits for cars, not just to cement the sale or to collect the small amount, but also to reinforce the purchase. The longer a customer has to wait for a car, the less he or she feels in control of the situation—and these doubts cause buyers remorse.

control of one's destiny—your job or your business for one

Control over one's destiny drives the at-home business phenomenon. It seems like everyone has a kitchen table or a garage business. People don't trust the corporate world anymore. They've seen too many people laid off from what was once a secure environment. Hot button marketers fill that void by selling turnkey businesses or franchises.

FedEx used to thrive on corporate business. Now it seems there's a FedEx truck on every street corner and in every rural area. Their slogan, "When it absolutely, positively has to get there overnight," used the Control Hot Button to create a zillion-dollar industry out of what was once a master's thesis.

American Express has a small business division, called "Open for Business," that concentrates on kitchen table industries. These days it seems everyone has a Web site where they're trying to sell something to somebody. Business machine manufacturers are making scaled-down versions of office equipment for such home entrepreneurs.

Check out the spam you receive via e-mail from people who are encouraging the short-sighted to start their own business with a "miracle in a box."

the jewish mother syndrome, or "what if?"

Whole industries have grown up on our desire to control the well-being of our loved ones. Check your neighborhood drug store and you'll find products that assure us we're raising our kids to be as healthy as can be. Michelin tires has created a franchise based on keeping the family safe rather than touting arcane tire specs. Volvo has built their whole franchise around the safety issue. Resealable plastic bags and single-portion packaging in foods are perfect examples of products that give buyers better control of their lives. And this also plays into the need of parents to ensure that everyone gets what he or she wants to eat—thus supporting the Family Values Hot Button as well.

Pampers capitalizes on the mother syndrome by taking it beyond caring for a baby. Nothing needs to be said when a Pampers commercial portrays a young mom interacting with her infant—then flashes forward to various times when the child is grown. The single message: "Are you doing the right thing for your baby's development?" It has a synergistic effect with the Nurturing Hot Button.

Some people also feel they're losing control when their house is disorganized or when they can't find things in their workspace. People want to control their environment as much as their personal well-being. An ordered world is a predictable world. Consider the fact that most people don't think they have enough closet or cabinet space. This lack of space makes them feel disorganized—and out of control. Enter the highly success-ful company California Closets. With all their brackets, hang-ers, and shelving, they built a nationwide business of creating storage space out of air—and satisfying their clients' Control Hot Button.

control over finances

Smart financial advisers sell security as much as wealth build-ing. The average homeowner is three paychecks away from getting deep in debt—or being forced to sell a home. Smart Realtors know that today people buy homes as much for their potential appreciation as for the warm family life they provide. But what if a homeowner does lose his or her job or a disaster occurs? Well, there's mortgage insurance. It's downright expensive when you compare it to other insurance policies, but it does give the homeowner a chance to get a good night's sleep and forget what could happen.

Big-ticket items can be a challenge for consumers. Consumers are frequently conflicted over their need to control versus their desire for change. Cars and houses are good examples. Consumers know they need to invest. They know they absolutely hunger for the new car or the new house. But they fear losing control of their financial equilibrium. Maybe they need to stretch their budgets several thousands beyond what they'd planned for to get what they want and need. How do hot button marketers handle that? Simple. They reduce the financial picture to the lowest denominator. Do you have any idea how many houses have been sold by a simple "You would be willing to give up a pack of cigarettes—or a single dinner out each week to have this gorgeous house to raise your children in, wouldn't you?" The smart hot button marketer knows that once things are presented in the lowest common denominator (even though cost remains the same), consumers regain their illusion of control.

control over relationships—getting them and keeping them

Our obsession with controlling relationships affects us in a great many ways, even in the purchase of a mundane sawhorse, as you saw in Chapter 3. A relationship doesn't necessarily mean marriage or love in the romantic sense, though that's how many people tend to think of it. Love for one's family, friends, and coworkers applies, too. It's all about our need to care deeply for other people—and feel cared for in return. Humans are social beings and, for the most part, abhor the vacuum of being alone. Just look at all the online dating services. In sales, we try to form a relationship and bond with our customers. Similarly, prospects look to the salesperson for respect and support. The loss of a relationship does not have to be physical. It can be emotional detachment from a loving spirit, too. Publishers capitalize on the need to fill that control void with self-help books that talk about how to feel good about ourselves even when we feel unloved and unworthy.

control over acquisitions

As mentioned, go into an electronics or appliance store like Best Buy and you might buy a $59 service warranty for a $79 appliance. Warranties are like life insurance for your purchases. We buy them to give us control and we hate to have to use them. Most appliance sellers make a great deal of money on warranties, because, as *Consumer Reports* says, warranties cost almost as much as the appliance. Warranties and guaranties only reinforce sales points. Nobody buys a product in hopes of returning it.

A purchase is also an extension of you. We are what we buy. When we show off our most expensive purchases to other people, we're looking for prestige (see the next chapter) and even one-upmanship. We show our status, longings, and interest through our purchases. Any good sales pitch should include the "your friends are going to envy you" implication. Most people will say they don't care. But they really do. Prestige is built on a relationship of one person feeling superior to another. People want to belong and feel accepted—on their own terms. A prestige product may be a great delineator, because the product can give buyers a feeling of control over how their peer groups feel about them.

the business of control

Companies rely on the Control Hot Button as much as consumers do. Companies prefer to stay with suppliers they can trust rather than shopping around. In the computer market, Michael Dell's Dell Computer has outlasted most of his competitors with a simple premise: "We're not selling anything hot and flashy, but you know what you're going to get—a reliable computer without fancy gizmos that break down."

One reason for Wal*Mart's incredible success is that they are *major* control freaks. They use computers to track each and every sale—even something as small as bubble gum, so they almost never run out of stock. They control all aspects of delivery and eliminate the middleman every time they can. They do their own warehousing. Wal*Mart controls deliveries and makes sure nothing sits too long. They make their manufacturers go to China to buy raw materials and labor so they can control costs. And, they don't work with unions, so they can control employee expenses.

how to control the control hot button

You have to build trust in making the current and future sale. Trust is a built-in understanding that goes beyond anything in a contract. Customers expect you to stay around before, during, and after the sale. A strong brand name is a symbol of trust and so is the persona of every smart hot button marketer. Moving from simply knowing your customers to building customer relationships and managing these relationships increases profits. It is the cornerstone of a hot button marketer.

- Stay in control of the selling situation, from beginning to end—and even after the sale.
- If you're making a sales call, don't allow the customer to call back. Set up a time you know you can reach her.
- Reassure your customer of others' satisfaction with stories almost identical to the buyer's circumstances.
- Be authoritative. Show the consumer you have his or her best interests in mind.
- Watch the body language to remove all doubts and to get at her true concerns.
- Build trust even before you make the sale.
- Show checkpoints and delivery times so she feels she's in charge.
- If you're selling a packaged product, use your entire package and the product to remind the customer that what she's purchasing is well worth the money.
- Play up the control factor in all advertising.
- Remember, in order to sell or market a product, you have to reassure the customer four times:
  1. When she sees the product on the shelf
  2. When she pays for the product at the checkout stand
  3. When she uses the product
  4. When she consumes the product (make her want more of the same?)

- Manage expectations wisely.
- Deliver exactly what's promised.

An axiom of business is to always give more than the value received, but if you deliver too much, the buyer will get suspicious. Don't oversell. When the delivery falls short of expectations, it will be very hard to win trust again. And trust is critical to making the consumer's need for control work in your favor.

pushing the hot button

for marketers

- Create long-term warranties for your product and back them up. Remember, a warranty is an insurance policy for the buyer.
- Don't play salesperson roulette with consumer or business clients. It makes the buyer feel that he or she is not in control, and has to learn new personalities and rebuild trust.
- In a volatile price situation, create plans, if possible, for customers to lock in prices for the long range, and assure on-time delivery.
- Identify customer expectations for service and product performance and link the delivery of the quality to specific tasks.
- Create products that can help consumers develop new revenue streams or at least ensure that the money keeps flowing in. For instance, tell a person how he or she can make money off an expensive new computer by opening up a word processing or desktop publishing business.

- Tell the buyer that you, personally, will oversee every aspect of the project. Keep the relationship going.
- Demonstrate, through concrete facts and figures, how your product will help your customer control some facet of his life.
- Keep your relationship going through the life of the project. Customers base the quality control, sales management, and functional quality of a product on the quality of interpersonal communications they have with you.
- In selling a business service, touch base with the customer at least once a week, even if you have to make up an excuse to call. Customers thrive on staying in the loop.

chapter 6

i'm better than you

what marketers need to know

The I'm Better Than You Hot Button is part of every culture. In effect, it appeals to the inner bully in all of us—which has few acceptable outlets in our adult lives. This hot button is not inherently good or bad, but is an important dynamic for some people. It feeds their self-esteem. It affects the consumer's decision-making processes regarding product, brand, and service selections.

The implications are significant for marketers. If a prestige brand is experiencing a declining level of cache or distinction, marketers and salespeople must identify and concentrate on the specific factor that is weakening the product image. You can change the advertising message, focus on the perceived value, and emphasize benefits of your brand versus competing brands.

People buy prestige products and services to communicate that they are better than the next guy or are equal to the peer group they aspire to be with. The I'm Better Than You Hot Button is much more than an appeal to snobbism. It has a social function. It is a reflection of your consumer's need to belong or fit in.

how marketers can apply this

Smart hot button marketers understand how critical the use of language is when they're trying to tap into their customer's hot buttons. So, they use loaded words to express prestige within their industry. You may not necessarily use the word "prestige," for example, but all the language you use needs to reflect what it is you're trying to sell to your client. Take the high road when you sell to status seekers. Unless your product has just been introduced or is a real rarity, they already know the what and the where. They need to know the which. For example, water is water, but people who want a prestige water may choose it over all the other waters in the store. Consumers know about Evian and where to get it, but it's up to marketers to sustain the prestige factor so that consumers will continue to cherish the brand. The table on the following page presents some prestige words that might fit.

what is prestige?

Groucho Marx was once asked about joining a certain country club. His now famous rejoinder was, "I wouldn't join any club that would have me as a member." They say all men are created equal. But they're not. At least they don't want to be. The desire for a higher status is universal. The status appeal is not only related to people. In the animal kingdom there is usually an "alpha" animal that has dominance or elevated social status, so to speak, within its pack. Status is an overwhelming opportunity. When you sell your product on its status appeal, you are implying that the competition is weak or inferior—and only the riff-raff will buy their products. And, of course, you get to make higher profits because there's almost always a higher price

*Prestige Words**				
aristocratic	elite	gracious	patrician	unique
blue blood	esteemed	honorable	prominent	upper class
crème de la crème	exclusive	impressive	quality	upscale
dignity	gentility	nobility	society	venerable
distinctive	gentry	outstanding	state of the art	who's who

*Have fun with your thesaurus, font selections, and colors (especially gold, silver, and bronze).

attached to status products. A high price can actually become part of the perceived value of a status product or service. People assume it's better quality simply because it's more expensive.

Some people label the I'm Better Than You Hot Button as "conspicuous consumption." For the most part, that's what it is. Others might call it "the art of living well." Still others say, "Living well is the best revenge." Whatever you call it, our second hot button uses outside means to impress others. Its major use is demonstrating or communicating a person's class or wealth.

The overwhelming method of choice for gaining status is buying goods and services. People are willing to pay dearly to enhance themselves in the eyes of their peers. The product should have emotional value as well as functional utility. Status seekers are not just buying summer homes, they're buying the kind of prestige, privileged privacy, and exclusivity that's found in out-of-the-way places like North Carolina's Hilton Head Island, a classy resort town.

This penchant for the best is (obviously) predictable among those in the upper strata of the income bracket. However, the poor also seek to distinguish themselves by buying goods that are above their class—as long as they are items that are highly visible and impressive to peers.

Liquor companies have long known this. Vodka, for example, is, by definition, neutral and tasteless. Yet research shows that consumers—especially in low-income areas—will go for the name brand in spite of the high price. Cadillacs, once considered prestige cars, are now favored in lower and lower middle class neighborhoods. Some working-class people will go for less-expensive, yet more showy forms of ostentation. I was told by one working-class person, "My friends may spend $500 on a junk heap, but outfit it with $2,000 shiny chrome hubcaps that spin."

Prestige is not only about goods—it's about services, too. Services that help prestige-seeking consumers position themselves above their peers are in high demand these days. According to the American Personal Chef Association, Americans employ about 9,000 personal chefs today, a significant increase above

marketing insight   Smart hot button marketers have a new market to target. It's a new population group called "the elite elderly," usually from their seventies on up. These are seniors who are into big-ticket items. They are active, like to go places, and enjoy showing off their acquisitions and their mobility. They buy extravagant watches to signal to others that they've "arrived." They buy high-profile items—like Cartier jewelry, watches, and accessories, alexandrite gemstones (the choice of royalty), A. Testoni shoes, Adirondack Reflections Beaver Blankets and accessories, handcrafted Alante Original Furniture, maybe a piano once owned by Liberace or Elvis Presley. In short, anything that they feel will impress others and allow them to improve, or at least keep up their social ranking.

the 400 that were employed just ten years ago. Consumers look for personal shoppers to buy their groceries, concierge services to run errands and book theater tickets, nannies to look after the kids, and masseuses to ease aching bodies and spirits.

And, these consumers tell family, friends, and acquaintances about these oh-so-special services. They talk about how much they need the services. They compare notes about how good—or bad—the service is. They even talk about the cost of the services. Cost is an essential part of the prestige factor. The more expensive, the better. One reason for prestige services is that it can be hard to be showy these days. Almost anyone can afford prestige products with the help of credit lines and credit cards. Distinguishing who has true wealth (versus dangerous levels of debt that they could never pay off in three lifetimes) is not as easy as it was in the past.

status and marketing

It's up to you as a hot button marketer to show how your product or service can enhance the buyer's status in other people's eyes. The obvious and external reason for traveling first class on an airplane is the extra legroom and creature comforts. But here's something the airlines won't tell you. Creature comforts aren't really all that special anymore. It's the internalized I'm Better Than You Hot Button that drives the sale. The people in first class get to watch the other people stumble and trip over themselves to get to the back of the plane and stow their luggage. First class even has a special lavatory that is reserved for the eight or fewer people usually sitting in first class. Is there a logical reason for this? Of course not. It's just a way to make the people in first class feel special and pay more.

Status seeking is a dynamic that is part of every culture. It's an invisible hand that drives consumers. However, what is perceived as status varies from consumer to consumer. Thus, the ways you reach varying market segments are as different as night and day. Take the sales of upscale sound systems. Granted, there is a functional benefit to good sound; however, there is also a psychosocial benefit in buying the most expensive stereo or sound system. It practically screams, "I'm a connoisseur!" Bang & Olufsen, the audio and video manufacturer, has been making upscale sound systems for years, with sleek designs that shout, "I'm rich." The more upscale it looks, the better it seems to sound—and all the better to show off.

people won't admit they want status

Despite the prevalence of the I'm Better Than You Hot Button there is a conundrum at work here—and it needs to be worked into your sales pitch. Most people simply won't admit to buying a product on status appeal. They usually rationalize their purchase on some other basis. When it comes to luxury cars, people rationalize the expense by talking about its wonderful engineering. In some cases that may be true, but consider that Cadillacs and Oldsmobiles used to be identical cars that came off the same assembly line.

Women may talk about how wonderfully well-designed and constructed Coach purses are. Are Coach purses that much better than others? It doesn't matter. The buyer sees the Coach logo and *perceives* the purse as better than others.

For status seekers, bragging rights come with the territory. Not only do status seekers buy "the best," but they may talk about how much "the best" cost them as well. The logic is simple: visibility is a cultural as well as a physical property. If neighbors talk about how expensive their new car, stereo, or handbag is, it becomes more conspicuous. The more conspicuous a product, the sooner it is noticed. And being noticed is what the I'm Better Than You Hot Button is all about.

In every status brand there is an "aura factor." The aura of the product bestows "borrowed prestige" on its owner. When they show off prized possessions, users transfer the perceived image of prestige into the feelings they hold about themselves—sort of like a security blanket.

For many people, buying is all about status and class distinction. Is this wrong? "It is a basic part of human nature," says one psychologist who researches consumer decision-making. "What is critical is the idea that not everybody can have it." Traditionally, the display is the point: people who don't know you will not know how intelligent or accomplished you are, but they can instantly see that you can afford more than they can.

price your product high

High price and relative unattainability confer a degree of exclusivity for a product or service—which in effect makes a well-known brand an aspirational symbol that people dream and strive to have. Mercedes has traditionally used price to try to protect the brand from commonness. Prestige pricing refers to setting an artificially high price for the product. The price tells consumers that the product is not for everyone, just the chosen few. The pricing evokes perceptions of quality and prestige for the product or service. When you want to imply status, the high price you set for a product or service is itself an important motivation for consumers. Consuming high-status products is viewed as a sign of wealth. The high, self-discriminating price enhances the value of the product or service. Several researchers have demonstrated that the price of products may play a positive role in determining the perception of quality.

status is self-rewarding

Self-esteem is in the eye of the individual. Individuals aspire to maintain positive thoughts about themselves. Consumers who buy on status and to enhance their self-esteem have a unique lens. They typically filter out the negatives of a product. They see the positives but hide the negatives—sometimes even to themselves. Why? Because talking or even thinking about negatives is a threat to how they want to perceive themselves—being better than everyone else.

Prestige products and services don't create status as much as they fulfill a consumer need for showing off. As with most hot buttons, consumers aren't aware that they are buying products based on snob appeal, which is what status really is. In fact, many consumers will deny that and create rationalizations to justify their purchases. For that reason, when marketers appeal to this status hot button they need to make their appeals subtle

marketing insight   Goods and services are not simply vehicles of utility: they serve an expressive function. What counts is what the goods say, not what they do. In modern societies goods are means of communication. They constitute a system of "signs" through which a purchaser makes statements about himself or herself. While in the old days goods only informed about social status, today they signal allegiance to a particular lifestyle.

and focus on the benefits. For many people, status products are part of the "extended self." The products can be cars, boats, or jewelry. The products define who we are or, at least, how we would like others to see us. The hope is that the strength and stylishness of a car will "rub off" on the owner.

You also shouldn't think that the I'm Better Than You Hot Button is only for adults. Beginning at about age seven and continuing well into their teens, children are very sensitive to brands used by their friends. Status seeking and self-esteem are what causes a child to favor a particular product. "My friends have/use it," so the thinking goes, "I want to be accepted by my friends. I must have it, too." It's all about being "in" with their peers. If the trendsetters in their peer group stop using the product, most of the time kids will choose other brands to enhance themselves.

benchmarks of a status sell

The selling of a Rolls-Royce is somewhat of an oxymoron. You don't sell Rolls-Royces. People buy them. The salesperson takes orders. Most of us don't have the luxury of owning a Rolls-Royce or a Ferrari. Most of us can't afford to buy a $150 bottle of wine. But we can use some of the same hallmarks to add status appeal to our product. Here's how:

- The product should be an example of conspicuous consumption but, paradoxically, it can fulfill a person's private moments. For instance, a fine wine consumed in the evening while reading a good book. We call these prestigious products that are reserved for special moments "little luxuries."

- The product or service should only be available to a "chosen few." You must learn the wants and psychological needs of your target market. The Prius may be a status car for the upper-middle-class person in midlife, but not so for many working-class Hispanic teens or twenty-somethings who take great pride in showing off their lowriders—old cars with specially equipped hydraulics that raise (the higher the better) and lower the cars at the push of a button. Good lowriders are hard to come by.
- Aesthetic appeal helps determine brand selection. Yes, the gold logo displayed on some luxury cars has a sort of aesthetic appeal to status-seeking consumers.
- The products should be sold on technical superiority, even if there is no great consumer benefit. People love to show off the gee-whiz bells and whistles of their purchases. Status seekers like to think they're on top of "the wave."
- A high price infers a higher level of quality and suggests a certain degree of prestige. "My cleaning person charges $200 to clean my house, but she's worth every penny" or "My Jenn-Air oven cost me $2,000 but the baking is first-rate."
- The product, and how it's positioned, should put consumers on a pedestal. When pricing products, you can readily appeal to the need to be better than others by keeping prices high and building up intrinsic value by limiting availability.
- Advertisements and promotional strategies should initially draw attention to rationalizations that allow consumers to pay the high price. They should also appeal to buyers who want to feel better than anyone else.

Prestige is like value. It is not what you put into a product; rather, it's what consumers take out of it. Society has set certain boundaries of good taste and prestige. But here's the weird part. The product does not have to be super in quality. We might assume that a low level of quality would be a big negative in determining prestige. But that's not nearly as important as the buyer perceiving the brand as having an excellent level of quality, whether it does or not. According to a major consumer magazine, many kitchen ovens bake at the same quality as a Jenn-Air. And then there's the old joke about Harley-Davidsons looking so good on the side of the road when you're trying to fix them.

Want more proof? Consider that these days it seems like everybody's on some kind of diet or cutting out carbohydrates, calories, etc. But Häagen-Dazs, Ben & Jerry's, and all of the other super-rich, super-butterfat, carbohydrate-laden, cardiac-blocking ice creams are selling well. The ability of humans to rationalize their prestige pleasures is endless when hot button marketers help them create the excuses. Whether people think the ice cream products are richer, creamier, better-tasting, or more natural, buying a prestige dessert makes a person feel better about him or herself. It even makes the ice cream taste better.

how the sales cycle works

Status seekers look for and place a high value on items that are in limited supply and are not in high demand. For instance, when the videotape recorder was introduced, very few people would buy it. When everyone had one, the status seeker jumped to a new electronic wizardry of choice. Products that are readily available have lesser "showoff" value, while those that are less available are more desirable. When a product is scarce, it has an even greater effect on demand if people also perceive the product as unique, popular, and expensive. Thus, status seekers have a need for uniqueness.

where do status seekers get their ideas?

People often get their ideas about living from their peers. However, status seekers, more than other consumers, also look to images in the media—particularly paid print and television advertising, or upscale "wish list" magazines such as the *Robb Report*—to learn about affluent lifestyles. They attempt to imitate stereotypes by using similar products. But paid commercials are just the beginning. People also get these stereotypes by watching TV shows and movies that construct their social reality. The consumer tries to become the character portrayed on TV. There was a movie some years ago called *Nurse Betty*, where the protagonist became so involved with a particular soap opera that she thought she was the main character. Most people don't go that far, but they personalize the messages that seep out through the media. So, if their favorite upscale character uses a certain product, they feel the need to use it, too.

This is somewhat different from previous generations—particularly prior to 1950. Back then, because of the lack of television and the Internet, there was (comparatively speaking) little exposure to the outside world. Therefore, people generally learned about status by observing their neighbors. Back then, it was a question of being better than the Smiths across the street. Today, the comparative factor bridges all levels of society. Today, there are many windows to the worlds of the rich and famous that mirror back magnificent images that consumers aspire to and to which they compare themselves.

hot button marketers should reflect the products they sell

This concept is important in selling but it is critical when you are trying to appeal to the I'm Better Than You Hot Button. You, as much as your product or service, become a facet of what your customer is buying. Whether your customer is striving to appear better than others in regard to intelligence, wealth, or style, you must reflect that back to them in how you dress, speak, and market yourself. You become part of the brand you represent. When selling status, hot button marketers have to be an extension of the products and services they sell.

- Your office and the way you dress must mirror the status image you're selling. Xerox, for instance, requires their repair people to dress in suit and ties, even though it actually hinders their work. But the people they sell to have certain expectations about professionalism and the way professionals should dress—which is in a suit and tie. Xerox asks their repair people to blend into the corporate environment. Prestigious salespeople do the little extras that establish a relationship with the products or services they're selling.
- The whole sale has to be an implied: "This is what you'll achieve by having this product (or service)." For example, you're going to have a different person selling a Jaguar than you would a Hyundai. In fact, a mismatch between the salesperson and the product—a misfit in the image embodied by the salesperson compared with the advertised message of the

consumable—is a common cause of missed sales in luxury items.

This I'm Better Than You strategy works best, of course, when the product is one that is readily visible to the public. It's not going to work quite so well for home utilities, underwear, or earplugs. The I'm Better Than You Hot Button can be coupled with the snob effect. It also can be complex because it can be influenced by other individuals' behaviors. The buyer reasons, "I want this particular salesperson, product, shop, or service because upscale peers are using him, her, or it."

pushing the hot button

for marketers
- Place your product in upscale outlets. The transfer of the luxury cachet happens at luxury stores and high-priced boutiques.
- Advertise in upscale magazines where people get their status ideas.
- Try to get your product placed in movies and TV shows that depict people with an upscale lifestyle.
- Don't be afraid to discount. According to Pamela Danziger, in her book *Why People Buy What They Don't Need*, the majority of people bought their last luxury product at a discount. Even the elite purchaser wants to save money.

for salespeople
- Play on the brand's affinity. Stress that only a certain type of person buys this type of product.

- Sell the experience of the product, not just the physical details.
- Prestige will presell the product or brand to your customers. Don't oversell, except for pointing out prestigious detailing it may have or the rarity and fine quality of the materials that went into it.
- Take careful note of how a person dresses. If a prospect is holding a $1,000 Gucci handbag, she sure doesn't want to pull a cheap wallet out of it.

chapter 7

the excitement of discovery

what marketers need to know

If boredom pushes us away from doing nothing, it is curiosity that pulls us toward investigating and acquiring new things. "Look what I found" is an exclamation of joy. Consumers who respond to the Discovery Hot Button want to discover everything by themselves. People are always on the outlook for new products. They will welcome your new product. And, they really do want to hear your new pitch, especially when you are presenting a new way to solve an old problem and promise to give them a way to discover something. The Discovery Hot Button is similar to the I'm Better Than You Hot Button—first and foremost, the joy is internal, because a discovery makes the consumer feel unique.

how marketers can apply this

It's relatively easy to enhance your product when you factor in "discovery" points. Simply give your product a new benefit the other guy hasn't thought of yet or add an extra unit of value.

Discover is one of the most powerful words in the human language. It has a host of synonyms that you can use to produce strong motivating ads and sales pitches (see the table on the following page). These words are far more than bromides used in advertising. They bring increased attention to almost any

speaking to discovery		
at last	improved	original
discover	innovative	secret
find	introducing	state of the art
finally	learn	uncover
Grand Opening	now	! → * (*symbols*)
new (*the most important of all*)		

new product or positioning. The keywords that you can elicit from customers when making a sale are "I didn't know that!" The successful hot button marketer leads customers in the right direction to make a new, cool discovery purchase by using the keywords and showing them things they didn't know before.

the quest for the unexpected

Let's face it. There aren't a heck of a lot of opportunities to discover things these days—not for humans without major bionic alterations anyway. Most of our discoveries are made with zillion-dollar telescopes, cameras, and spacecraft. But there are a great many discoveries that can fulfill consumer needs. A discovery is something learned or found—it includes both the new and the unexpected. New products and services—and new uses for familiar products—are a delight because they allow consumers to, once again, enjoy the thrill of discovery.

Avon's Skin So Soft was found to be effective at repelling bugs. The discovery of this new use traveled quickly from customer to customer, and sales actually spread faster than if Avon had released a new bug repellant. People were thrilled to find this unexpected new use.

To paraphrase what noted physicist Stephen Hawking has said (only he made his statement in the context of science, not marketing), "Discovery may not be better than sex, but the satisfaction lasts longer." People love "discovering" new things and usually want to tell others about their discoveries. Sometimes they tell everyone, as in the case of the Avon product. Sometimes they tell a chosen few. This is what referral marketing is about. Businesspeople like referring good, newly found venders to others. Discoverers are referred to as "early adopters" in marketing textbooks, but this is much too simplistic. People in every demographic grouping are in search of new pleasures.

Consumers want to discover a great new vacation spot but they don't necessarily want everyone to know about it. They sometimes find a grand, new glorious place to live and want to bar the doors from any new visitors. Frequently you'll hear residents say, "You're welcome to come for a visit . . . but don't stay." In this case, the discovery is "our little secret." It's also a great marketing ploy when used to sell travel or vacation homes; we all know the draw of the "vacation hideaway."

Discovering something new and different makes a person feel exclusive and smart. Discoverers feel that their unique knowledge sets them apart in their peer group and that in turn raises their self-esteem. I know a person who discovered a new caffeinated mint, available only on the Internet. He takes great delight in giving one to people in his car and then watching the look of amazement on their faces when they pop the mints into their mouth. They're amazed that they can get the extra caffeine-aided burst of energy in a good-tasting mint. The payoff is when his friends say, "This is great! Where did you find it?"

discovery lives in the mind of the beholder

So what is a discovery? A discovery is the end result of curiosity. Everyone has his or her own idea of what a discovery is. For some, it's finding a new way to do things faster, better, or cheaper. For a collector of coins, it might be finding a rare nickel. For an investor, it might be a new way to predict movement in the stock market or an underpriced "For Sale By Owner" home. A discovery can be either a private matter that satisfies a hidden want (it's up to the marketer to find that hidden want) or a public display of prestige.

A discovery is a doorway that leads to the unknown. It can lead to a new idea, a new way of life, a changing way of life, a new way to do things—but it's always, by nature, unexpected. In short, a discovery is a surprise.

Discoverers will frequently spend a few hours—or whole days—wandering through secondhand bookstores looking for a little-known book or taking in the one-of-a-kind offerings at the local flea market. But they can also be found flipping through newspapers and magazines. Years ago, during a newspaper strike, people were asked what they missed most about not having their newspaper. The most common answer was the Sunday ads. Readers liked discovering all the new products and ways to do things they had not seen before.

At the time of this writing, Gillette is introducing a battery-operated vibrating razor. People are buying it in hopes of discovering a better way to shave. They're also trying to make the mundane fun. Hope plays a big part of the discovery process, as you'll see in the "Risk and Reward" section later in this chapter.

It's always fun to discover something yourself—without anyone's input. Usually, though, there is an "enabler" involved. The enabler is the guide or the salesperson who shows you how to discover that unexpected pleasure or leads you in the right direction. The Internet, for example, is built on discovery. It is a limitless universe of information. Search engines are the enablers. More than 80 percent of Web finds are the result of using search engines. Yahoo!, in fact, was built on the Discovery Hot Button. A couple of college students discovered some interesting and intriguing sites on the Internet and made a list that expanded geometrically as they found links to more and more sites. The success of Yahoo! is a testament to the power of the Discovery Hot Button.

the bandwagon effect, reversed

The Discovery Hot Button has one drawback. Sales based on discovery can be fragile. You can only make the discovery once. It's like when you discover a little-publicized movie, and your peers are impressed that you found it. But here's the rub. When a secret becomes mainstream, the original discoverers tend to jump off the bandwagon. This is a very common backlash so, as a hot button marketer, you have to milk the sales on the fly. That's why sleeper TV shows (unexpected and unpublicized hits) usually flop or become unpopular after the first two years or so. The discoverers abandon it. It's not hip anymore. The discovery factor is gone. It's no longer unique. Hey, if everyone knows about the show, it's not a secret. That's why you have to keep surprising customers with new "hip" products and benefits.

The market is built on novelty and discovery. We even create hybrid dogs to sell on the discovery principle—but new breeds usually fall out of favor when the secret is tossed aside and the breed reaches mainstream popularity. This year's "must have" dog is the Goldendoodle. Yes, really! It's a cross between a golden retriever and a poodle. It may quickly fade in popularity as the Peekapoo did. Hey, there was a time that mixed-breed dogs were called mutts, right? Don't tell the breeders who make a living discovering new breeds. That's our little secret.

the secret society

A trick to pushing the Discovery Hot Button is to keep it a secret or to give the impression that it is a secret. Most people now know about putting Arm & Hammer Baking Soda in the refrigerator. But it got there via the Discovery Hot Button. Here's how it happened.

Arm & Hammer's advertising agency was trying to find new markets for baking soda. They interviewed groups of consumers. One of the people interviewed said she used the baking soda to keep odors down in the fridge. The creative people listening in the backroom thought they had reached nirvana. They created a commercial that shouted, "Put Arm & Hammer in your refrigerator to neutralize odors." Viewers were underwhelmed. The agency was at a loss. They couldn't understand what had gone wrong. They went back and reviewed the commercial with the lady who suggested the new usage. She told them their approach had been completely off base. You don't shout that you have odors in the refrigerator, she told them. She explained that you place the box in back of the refrigerator where no one can see. She said it was a secret that only a few people knew about.

So, the agency went back and revised the ad. The new approach was "*Psssst*. Got a secret. Put a box of Arm & Hammer in back of your refrigerator to keep your refrigerator smelling great." The keyword was "secret." Consumers loved the discovery of a new use for an old favorite. And, because it was placed in back of the refrigerator where no one but the user would see it, it remained a secret.

The point is that discoverers like to keep secrets and find new ways of doing things. It makes them feel special. Discovery can also be fun. After the Arm & Hammer commercial aired, marketers came up with products to disguise the product further, like little plastic birds that decorated and fought odors. Arm & Hammer itself kept adding new features to the product to keep the product appeal going and going.

risk and reward

Selling on the Discovery Hot Button requires a different approach than most of the other hot buttons. But it combines the benefits of the other hot buttons. For instance, people may discover a new way to control their lives. People may find a new status symbol, and as we mentioned, discovering is a status-enhancing hot button when people show off their new products to their peers. But here's the difference. Unlike most purchases where consumers want a win-win situation, discovery welcomes a bit of risk. There is a direct correlation between the risk and how much physical or psychological reward the prospect hopes to get. The reward of finding a new wine at a higher price can justify the mystery of what's in the bottle, behind the kooky little label. But there's even more risk involved than just the few dollars spent on the wine. What if you serve the wine to a group of friends and they don't like it?

So, when using the Discovery Hot Button to sell a product or service, you must reassure the customer that the reward far exceeds the risk. Of course, the Discovery Hot Button doesn't work for everyone, so you have to know your customer. People who are solely interested in staying within their comfort zone miss out on the joy of discovery—which restricts them to known products and services.

The joy of discovery usually won't work with a high-priced item like a car or a utilitarian item like a computer. In both these cases, the risk-reward factor is too great. Even so, discovery can

---

real-life example   You'd think that visitors to theme parks would pretty much know what they want to see and what they want to do. But, by and large, they don't. It's true. They may generally know that they'd like to ride a roller coaster or see a show. But frequently they find themselves at a loss of what to do—until they let the discovery impulse take over.

Theme parks are built on the illusion of discovery. In a well-designed theme park, you can't make a turn without discovering something new and different. In fact, in most theme parks you can't make a right-angle turn at all. You sort of curve into a diorama of discovery. Theme parks take us to imaginary worlds where we can discover lions in their natural habitat and roller coasters that let us discover space (Space Mountain in Disney World). But with every turn we discover something new and different.

help provide a justification or rationalization for the sale. How to use the risk-reward factor is illustrated in the following figure.

People also feel empowered when they discover something. They feel smart. When people move to a new city, they pride themselves on finding the hot areas or shortcuts for getting around all by themselves. We even learn better when we discover something without the help of someone else. Our self-confidence skyrockets when we discover something that no one else knows about—when we enter new worlds that other people have missed.

flea markets, costco, and wal*mart—theme parks all

Flea markets, Costco, and Wal*Mart are all venues that create a world of discovery for shoppers. Watch a salesperson selling a piece of jewelry at a local flea market. He or she will point out signatures, show you a certificate of authenticity, and even point out flaws to prove that you're looking at a one-of-a-kind item. And, have you watched the wide-eyed wonderment of shoppers at flea markets when they "discover" a treasure buried deep beneath a pile of bargains? In fact, if you watch, you may see that the first place people check out at a flea market is most often a box or a pile of items set off to the side.

One of Wal*Mart's tenets is that people want to discover something new. Look at the setup of a typical Wal*Mart aisle. First you find a basic, low-priced product in front of the aisle. It's usually a good, serviceable piece of merchandise—and a good value. But that's only the start of the sales process. You're cleverly led down the aisle to new products and new features—that are always more expensive than the featured item. Costco has become a family destination where shoppers consistently discover new products—many of which can't be found elsewhere.

When I run a focus group, the first question I ask is, "What new product did you try last?" I always get an answer. People genuinely enjoy finding and talking about new products, even if

real-life example   Shopping Networks on TV are crash courses in selling via the Discovery Hot Button. These shopping events are a very unique form of entertainment—with the serious focus on selling. More importantly, they appeal to shoppers who are very much drawn to the excitement of discovery when they shop. Every segment of the show features a new category of merchandise. People watch the show for hours and hours in the hope that they will find something new and different. The jewelry segment always seems to include a new gemstone with an unpronounceable name that is only found in a remote mine in Armenia. Never mind that the name, when translated, probably means "rock." The host's enthusiasm and the viewers' natural penchant for wanting to discover something both help suspend disbelief. Listen to the pitches on the various shows. Remember that shopping shows get instant feedback via phone calls, so they are always refining their pitches. Learn from them.

they don't always like them. It seems that people enjoy the hunt as much as the product itself. That's one of the reasons many restaurants get good traffic when they are first opened. However, after the discovery, it's up to the restaurateur to make sure the restaurant is worth going back to a second or third time.

discovery and the $500 rule

The new product business is totally based on discovery. That's why new products are so exciting to consumers. The joy of discovery ensures that almost any new product or service will generate at least passing interest. Why do consumers prowl supermarket aisles instead of just grabbing the one product they need? They're hoping to discover something unique. Babies will coo in delight when they discover something new. Teenagers will embrace a discovery when it separates them from their parents and meets with the approval of their peers. Grownups will be delighted to discover something that enhances their lives in a new way. All these will add to your bottom line when you hit the hot button of discovery.

One marketer has a unique rule that tells him his customers are ripe for the Discovery Hot Button. He looks at how much money a person has invested in a particular interest and how enthusiastic that person is about this interest. Anyone who has invested more than $500 in a special interest is ripe for a sales approach based on the Discovery Hot Button. For instance, if an individual has invested $500 in cookware, then he or she is ripe for new, unique cooking and gourmet items. If a person goes to a local pottery class and shows genuine enthusiasm for making things, then that person will surely want to discover new molds and greenware.

pushing the hot button

for marketers

- Use infomercials and the shopping networks. They always highlight something new and different. Use innovative-sounding titles like "New Product Discoveries."
- Use a dramatic design change, like today's tiny "flash drives" (which store a great deal of computer data but are the size of a lipstick case), that change the way consumers perceive the product.
- Use *new, new, new* in all your ads and on the package. It's a code word for discovery.
- Offer free trials or samples. If it's a software program, offer a free trial where a user can try out your product.
- Attempt to break the monotony of the everyday. Surprise the consumer and stimulate all five senses.

for salespeople

- Surprise a consumer (and above all, respond to the need for something unexpected) at least once a day, or even better, once a sales call.
- Create bargain bins without any kind of organization for consumers to rummage through. It allows them to feel they are "discovering" a new treasure.
- Get testimonials on how this new discovery changed a person's life.
- Take advantage of your existing customer base. Show current customers a new product that your company is introducing. They are likely to become the product's first customers and start word-of-mouth.

chapter 8

revaluing

what marketers need to know

The Revaluing Hot Button is a relatively new hot button that's just now coming of age. It's a hot button that will drive behavior and purchasing decisions in this country for the remainder of this decade and way beyond. Revaluers are a segment of the market that is self-motivated, self-directed, and self-focused. In the coming years they are going to be spending more money on self-enjoyment and personal luxuries. It's a lucrative market that will spend freely—if approached properly. But it's also very demanding.

how marketers can apply this

Do not sell to them. Allow revaluers to make their own purchasing decisions. Present opportunities to the revaluers and make it easy for them to continue staying involved at whatever level they choose. Speak to their value systems and strive to establish and build a level of trust that encourages a more customer-oriented, consultative relationship. Hot button marketers must learn to speak the language of the revaluer. It is a language of respect and accomplishment; however, never "talk down" to them. Above all don't use the hard-sell approach on revaluers or make the sales process complicated. Use a no-hassle approach. Revaluers won't put up with anything more—or less.

what and who are revaluers?

In the early fifties, they toddled. In the sixties they marched. During the seventies and eighties they built careers and families. Who are we talking about? Baby boomers. These baby boomers, now hitting their mid-fifties, are entering yet another phase in their lives. They're taking stock of their lives—revaluing.

Baby boomers were the first "Me Generation"—and they still are. On the whole, they aren't overly concerned with fixing all the problems of the world. They've done their stint. Finally, the boomers are saying, "This is my chance to be happy." At the same time they are reacting to a surprising phenomenon. They were taught that by working hard and living up to others' expectations in society and at work, they would ultimately achieve a comfortable retirement. Many have discovered that just isn't true. And, now, they're saying, "It's time to look after me and what I want, because apparently no one else is going to."

Boomers are beginning to think that looking to *past* comforts and happiness may help them find it in the present. They remember the places they ventured to in the past. They know what kind of travel they like and the places they like to go. They're returning to products and entertainment that offer them contentment and familiarity. This trend is largely responsible for the growing

marketing insight

Revaluers more often focus on the customer experience than on the product. Their desires are less material than in earlier life stages and more experiential. Many are eschewing narcissistic, acquisitive values that influenced them when they were younger. They now have a greater concern for their legacy, relationships, maintaining a purposeful existence for as long as they live, and in the well-being of the world's inhabitants. They are more likely to volunteer time and money on the causes that they think are near and dear to them.

success of Nick at Nite on Nickelodeon, with comfort programming like *The Mary Tyler Moore Show*, the *Dick Van Dyke Show*, and *Bewitched*.

Baby boomers will gravitate toward venues that are familiar, and therefore comforting, but often with a contemporary twist—say, a new way of traveling to a familiar place. These people also want greater control over their lives. They have learned that they have to look out for themselves and focus on what's important in their lives—family, financial security, and health.

Boomers have already "been there and done that." They've had to make hard decisions all their lives based on what they were told they should do. Now that they can—finally—invest freely and don't have families to support or bosses to answer to, they are insisting that they be allowed to make their own decisions.

If anything is certain in the world of sales and marketing, it's that the revaluing population is booming. Have those people changed? In physical ways, of course. The sixties rock group Cream had a reunion concert in London's Albert Hall in 2005. Reviewers remarked that most of the audience—and the band itself—looked like their grandparents. But mostly it's the emotional cues that have changed. Has this generation become more like their parents, as was once predicted, concerned with saving money for their retirement and living for their children? The answer is no, and yes. Am I being contradictory? Yes, and no.

how big is the market?

In 1900 there were 13 million people in the United States over the age of 45. *American Demographics*, in 1992, claimed that in the past decade, the 50- to 54-year-old age group grew by 55 percent, making it the fastest-growing age group. In 2004 there were nearly 100 million over 45, according to *Fast Company* magazine.

Between 2002 and 2012, almost 50 percent of the current work force will be eligible for retirement. They have the ways and the means to get what they want. Of course, as a marketer it can be downright foolish to pigeonhole a group of people that large. But based on my interviews and focus groups, you *can* find and take advantage of commonalities.

For one thing, the baby boomers are raging against aging. According to David Wolfe, president of Wolfe Resources Group, they are the most misunderstood generation in history. They won't allow themselves to grow old. They're getting out the wrinkle removers and hair and beard dyes. What's interesting is that few companies, outside of insurance companies and vitamin companies, have been marketing to this prime market.

PepsiCo admits that they have no marketing programs positioned to this demographic. Yet, these consumers have more wealth and are more brand loyal than any other age group. The *Chicago Tribune* is attempting to go after this market with a new magazine called *Satisfaction*. However, *Mature Adult*, Chicagoland Publishing's quarterly magazine for elderly readers, will cease publication this year because it didn't grow as quickly as was hoped. What's going on? It's really quite simple. Baby boomers don't want to be considered old. They see themselves as being in transition.

Instead of burning bras, they're burning their AARP (American Association of Retired People) cards. *Satisfaction* is a great title for a magazine, because it's what the revaluers want. *Mature Adult* doesn't appeal to revaluing boomers' desire for play.

Baby boomers are redefining the rules—just as they did in the sixties. Marketers make major mistakes by thinking that people will act like the generation before them. Baby boomers never have paid much attention to the rules. And, they're trying to redefine the facts of nature. The generation that at one time said "I won't wear makeup" now spends 20 percent more on makeup than the national average.

Are they denying youth or celebrating new values? Both. Boomers don't want to see themselves as having gray hair, because they feel like they're living exciting lives. Traditional fifty-plus products are likely to turn off a good portion of aging boomers. At the same time, they're spending more at health clubs and at health food stores. This is a good thing for marketers. It means that marketers don't have to consider products that appeal to younger consumers out of the running for the baby boomers.

Revaluers are a mixture of regret and anticipation. If they traveled as youths instead of saving their money, they regret not having saved. If they saved their money, they regret not having traveled and want to do it now. If they bought a very expensive oven in the past, they regret not having money for their future—which may include buying a very expensive oven. They're moving into smaller, more lavish properties filled with creature comforts like elaborate multimedia centers. And, in an attempt to simplify and improve the quality of their lives, baby boomers continue their exodus from urban locations to the Southwest, Florida, and Montana.

As baby boomers age and their children leave the nest, the divorce rate will continue to soar because "revaluing" baby boomers will put their personal happiness first and choose to end difficult marriages.

In this revaluing generation, "the children are more autonomous," said one person interviewed in a focus group. "I'll send them money, but they have to live for themselves. If they don't have the money, they'll have to go get it." I asked this woman if this wasn't a bit harsh. She said, "Yes, it is. And, of course, I'll help my kids. But they have to learn to make it on their own."

She's thinking about her own priorities—what's important to her. She wants to sell her luxurious home for a townhouse. She doesn't want to worry about, or hassle over, the school system. "I don't want land anymore because maintenance is part of having land," she said.

It's the "Me Generation" of the twenty-first century. The revaluing generation wants more free time. They want comfort above all else. They want to immerse themselves in their own interests. They want mental and cultural stimulation. Said another woman, "I believe the difference between me and my parents is that they considered their work was done and they waited around to die." Said yet another, "I want to see my new grandchildren but I don't want that to interfere with my class on feng shui."

While they won't repent for their age, revaluers would appreciate a bit of subtle help. When asked what she wanted in a new oven, one woman said, "The oven would say takeout. Since I do have to cook, I would ask for an ergonomically shaped oven. My knees don't work that great anymore."

Remember, if you're selling to this new revaluing generation, you can't talk about their arthritic knees. You have to imply their limitations very subtly: "Everything is at eye level." As baby boomers continue to revalue their lives, emotional connections to purchases should drive manufacturers to develop products and strategies that enhance the consumer's perception of a better lifestyle. The trend toward nutraceuticals—nutrient-based health products—is driven by baby boomers seeking preventive maintenance for aging bodies. However, marketers who sell the concept of using the product to preserve or enhance youth will have the greatest success.

revaluing—endings and new beginnings

In the United States, 50 percent of marriages lead to divorce, and 70 percent of second marriages end in divorce. Divorce is part of the growth sequence. It's a gateway to new values and role experimentation. After a divorce, many women and men can't believe they were with their partners as long as they were. "My God, there's freedom out there," they say. Many have grown leery of marriage and prefer to live with a partner—or alone. They are buying products for one or two, instead of a whole houseful of people. They want relationships but don't want to be controlled by a mate.

Revaluing is complicated, because revaluers come with a lot of baggage. For instance, the revaluing generation probably went to college and spent small fortunes on preschools, day schools, and any other educational things that were trendy at the time. But they haven't often received a payoff. Many feel they were sold a bill of goods. Their kids still have the same problems as any other generation. And, at the same time, stuck in midmanagement positions, they see companies hiring younger people above them. This is frustrating. So they look for new outlets where they can grow and be productive.

The revaluing generation had more disposable income than any generation in history. And they invested a great deal of this money in raising and educating their generation Y children. They're looking for, but don't expect, a payback. They now say, "You make your bed and you lie in it." Many revaluers now feel the only sure financial or emotional investment is in themselves.

Some made bad choices in marriages and swear that it won't happen again. Said a revaluing baby boomer, "This is my time to be selfish. I don't necessarily like that, but I made bad choices in my life. Changing myself is a process and it's not going to happen overnight."

If you check into the habits of revaluers, they're among the highest percentage of people going back to school. Baby boomer enrollment at community colleges is soaring. Many boomers have saved money from the sale of a house and they're getting into new careers. Accountants are learning to be artists. Artists are studying to be accountants.

The revaluing generation is also downsizing. They're opting for smaller homes, condos, and even apartments. Because their children are leaving the nest, their home is now little more than a house—and an income-producing property. The attitude is more like "this is a place to live." Even so, these consumers aren't spending less money. They're demanding more creature comforts—home libraries may sit in the room next to the media center. Locales are more expensive and pricy. Lots are

marketing insight

Baby boomers don't want to wait any longer; after all, they were the first people in 1,000 years to see a millennium end and a new one begin. They want their pleasures now. This could explain why direct-mail campaigns to boomers usually draw a lackluster response—and why shopping on the Internet has become so strong. The Internet is immediate gratification—no muss, no fuss. Click, give a credit card number, and your purchase is at your door in two days or so. Likewise, point-of purchase advertising tends to work well because it provides the quick hit.

smaller—and still the dream for many is a fully maintained home on the golf course. At the same time, the typical home is not as flashy as the days when they were young. They don't need all the flash and glitz—comfort and elegance are the watchwords. Revaluers want to be comfortable. If they can find an apartment that meets their needs, fine. They are trading size for amenities.

small breaks, big pleasures—major hot buttons

Big pleasures for baby boomers come in small doses. A "beverage moment" is a major break for them. Marketers who put coffee bars in Borders bucked the odds and broke all the marketing rules. Instead of using their in-store real estate to pile up more and more books and CDs, they created a great space for a revaluative moment. Consumers can sit and read magazines and the latest books for the price of a latte. And if the store has a wireless Internet connection to search the Web, all the better. There is a chain of coffee shops in the Albuquerque area called Flying Star. I must admit, I've written many portions of this book there—yes, over a Latte Grande. I asked one of the employees how the Internet and the magazines on the rack behind me had affected business. Her response, "Business went from good to great."

Venues like Flying Star, Starbucks, and Borders can be called comfort stops, and the baby boomers look forward to these precious, low-hassle moments.

marketing insight

As baby boomers continue to revalue their lives, emotional connections to purchases should drive hot button marketers to develop products and strategies that enhance these consumers' perceptions of a better lifestyle, such as educational toys for grandchildren and healthier foods.

The Revaluing Hot Button is responsible for the rise in health and beauty care products. If shown reasonable, reasons-why proof, both women and men want to try the new skin regenerating products. Of course, the products may or may not work, but if they do, the revaluing consumers feel they can stave off the effects of aging just a little bit longer. They are also a big market for bath soaps and gels, because revaluers are very into self-enjoyment and little luxuries. In fact, the revaluers are more into self-enjoyment than self-achievement. They are spending more on themselves. They want to pamper themselves. "This is *my* time. I've spent twenty years raising kids and now I'm looking out for me," they say. Revaluers find it very easy to rationalize self-involved purchases.

Baby boomers gravitate toward products that are familiar—and therefore comforting—but often with a contemporary twist. They still buy their favorites like Cheerios, Captain Crunch, and Fruit Loops, but they want these older flavors to have a new interpretation, such as Frosted Cheerios or Cinnamon Life. They want the current products to create the same emotion they remember from long ago. But, once again, this has to be implied, because they don't want to be treated like kids or as older people; they are adults. They want to know their cereal is high in nutrition but still has the familiar shapes they grew up with.

how do hot button marketers sell to revaluers?

You don't. You let them buy. You use the consultative selling approach. Because, more than other demographic groups, this generation buys on trust, according to Bud Holbert, a sales executive and trainer. Baby boomers have seen every kind of hard-sell approach and are weary of salespeople who push too hard. Don't base your sale on a low price, because these people like bells and whistles and have the money to satisfy their wants and desires. Revaluers want marketers to adjust to them, instead of vice versa. Remember, they were the "Me Generation" and got everything they wanted. Boomers have changed the ways cars are sold. When you sell to a baby boomer, it's no longer a "get 'em in the hot seat" approach that works. It's "How can we solve your needs with a minimum of hassle?" This isn't a generation fooled by marketing. They can see through the gimmicks. If you can't provide the appearance of real value, they see through it.

real-life example   There's a new kind of store in town. It's called the health food superstore. Consumers have the honor of paying almost twice as much for the identical product they'd find in a supermarket. Whole Foods is the best example of this type of store. As Costco has become a destination for the younger generation, Whole Foods has become a destination for revaluers. It offers samples so buyers can taste the products before they buy them. There are entire sections of enticing ready-to-serve meals, expensively priced, that people can take home as a dinner for one or two people. And, if the buyer wants a comfort moment, there are welcoming tables where consumers can sit and relax. Stores like Whole Foods and Wild Oats have become dating hot spots, where the revaluing generation can meet others like themselves without the hassles of singles bars—which the revaluing generation has eschewed because they are just too noisy for their aging ears.

The aisles at Whole Foods and Wild Oats are wide and easy to negotiate. They're like adult theme parks where each turn brings the consumer new items to discover. The stores are staffed by knowledgeable employees who go out of their way to please the customer. All of these perks remind consumers how personal service used to be when they were young. Compare this to the "herd—them—in—get—them—out" mentality of the typical supermarket and you can see why revaluers are willing to pay premium prices.

use a no-hassle approach

The revaluing generation doesn't want to be hassled anymore. They take pride in their knowledge and refuse to be talked down to by incompetent, inconsiderate salespeople using bogus or canned sales pitches. These shoppers have experience, education, and a pocketbook that's hard to beat. Traditional advertising and an aggressive sales approach doesn't work with these people. They don't want to be talked at; they want to be talked to.

One direct-mail advertiser tells about a marketing campaign he created some time ago and has since revised. It was a prospecting letter mailed to people ages forty-five to sixty-five. Originally the usual spiel was something along the lines of: "How would your family survive if you died tomorrow?" Today the approach has changed. The visual is a serene picture of grandparents taking their grandkids for a walk. When the new campaign was created, the company was looking for an 1.5 percent increase in response rate. But this particular revision netted a 24 percent return—selling to an audience who does not usually respond to direct-mail pitches!

To summarize, revaluers focus more often on the buying experience than on the product. Their not-so hidden desires are less for acquiring things, and are more experiential. Pleasures are more in the realm of little luxuries—enjoyment sought in little details of life. For many of us, the earlier part of life is about getting and keeping. Revaluers are different. They care about enjoying themselves. They have grown through self-realization and gained through self-confidence and self-sufficiency. This growth is an opportunity for marketers.

pushing the hot button

for marketers

- Develop products and strategies that enhance consumers' perception of a better lifestyle, such as educational toys for their grandchildren and healthier foods for themselves.
- Offer oldies and music reunions as premiums with your products.
- Offer timesavers. Revaluers' need to blindly acquire things is falling by the wayside. They are less likely to give up time for money.
- Use a cause-related marketing approach. These people grew up with Earth Days and the Vietnam War. They are ripe for a pitch that has a good cause, say donating a portion of money for the Special Olympics, embedded in the offer.

for salespeople

- Remind people of the good times they had—and can have again when going to a particular venue or using a product.
- Always use the consultative selling approach. Their needs for personal connection and security are key. Revaluers don't just buy a product; they embrace it—particularly for high-ticket items.
- Revaluers are liable to be skeptical and idealistic at the same time. Allay their fears, and if possible, overlay your sales pitch with doing something good for someone.

chapter 9

family values

what marketers need to know

According to most recent reports, including ones from Nickelodeon and WonderGroup, an advertising agency that specializes in kids and family marketing, the Family Values Hot Button may be the hottest of the hot buttons. In a recent study on developing and positioning a new fireplace insert, it was the vision of a family sitting in front of the hearth that turned on most consumers. Selling to the Family Values Hot Button can present challenges largely because the family unit is changing due to economics and time pressures of modern life. However, hot button marketers can readily sell to family values if they remember to sell to the family not as it is but as our consumers would like it to be. Family life as we know it is evolving, and marketers and salespeople are being called on to satisfy this hot button in new ways.

how marketers can apply this

There is a long list of business products and services that use the Family Values Hot Button. Perhaps the biggest name is Disney. Adding the name Disney to a product gives it a great deal of sales impetus. That's why Disney is so picky about its licensees. It's an overwhelming equity. But Disney World is not selling rides, or even a vacation. It's selling family values. That's what marketers need to know. When you get the family photos back from Cinderella's Castle, you'll probably forget about the long waits for the rides, the soda spilled on your favorite shirt, and the kids crying for more ice cream.

Consumers are also looking to re-create the image of family values by reproducing the types of food they remember from childhood. However, the meals and get-togethers consumers remember are idealized versions of the reality. Memories of childhood meals are firmly rooted in processed foods, not the made-from-scratch dinners of two generations before them. Sell to the ideal. Don't be afraid of getting too "schmaltzy." When researching a product, talk to Mom and to her kids. Sell the physical rewards to everyone in the family but, like Disney, sell the psychic rewards of family togetherness to the parents. When you talk about a prospect's family, the message is almost never as sappy as it sounds.

are family ties really different from the way they were?

"Children are out of control. They continue to defy their elders and rebel." While this remark could have come out of a New Age parenting magazine or the *Dr. Phil* show, it didn't. It's a paraphrase from a quote attributed to Aristotle over 2,000 years ago. The continuity and passion of family relationships is one of the strongest consumer motivations. Consider these, for example:

- A majority of fathers have witnessed the birth of their babies.
- Both men and women want a better relationship with their kids than they had with their parents.

- Women are still trying to be supermoms. Many women still get most of their joys from family relationships.

Unfortunately, today's vision of family togetherness is more a function of the media's treatment of family life than any reality. According to the book *Why They Buy*, by Robert Settle and Pamela Alreck, only one in twenty families fits the bill of a single marriage, two-parent, two-children household. Despite that, most consumers still want a quick fix to their family problems, like those they see in sitcoms. The family breakfast is dead and the family dinner is soon to be another casualty of modern life. Dinner was, at one time, a shared experience. Family members would discuss their daily events. But while 40 percent of American families share dinner at the end of the day at least once a week, the economics of the two-paycheck family means that at least one of the dinner providers is going to be too tired to do much cooking or socializing. That's why family-themed restaurants like Olive Garden and Red Robin have brought forth reasonably inexpensive "get-the-family-together dining."

Our family values and the ways we satisfy them are a series of tradeoffs. We've traded family dinners for "quality time" with the kids in the car as we chauffer them to soccer games and gymnastics. "Soccer Mom" has become part of our everyday vocabulary. In fact, it is even in the dictionary. Dictionary. com defines it as "An American mother living in the suburbs whose time is often spent transporting her children from one athletic activity or event to another." ("Soccer Dad" isn't in the dictionary . . . *hmmn* . . . what does that say about our roles?) We're swapping informal gatherings of kids for formal, planned play dates. The family room, which was once a place for family activities and social bonding, is now a multimedia center or a shared space for compartmentalized living.

the ideal family doesn't exist, and never has

There is trouble in familyland, but there always was. So where do consumers get their vision of family values? From today's multimedia world. The consumer's vision of togetherness is more a factor of the media's treatment of family life than anything based on reality. Reruns of *Leave It to Beaver* and *The Brady Bunch* have left their mark. They define our ideal of family life. Beaver's and Wally's big crises came when Wally couldn't get a prom date or when Beaver tried to hide a newfound frog from his mom. If only our own problems were that small.

marketing insight

A study done by TV Land and Nick at Nite has found that families that consistently dine together and focus on one another at mealtime are more likely to describe themselves as very satisfied with the closeness of their families.

Quality time with families is still of utmost importance to Americans. But the traditional family is more myth than actuality. As mentioned, marketing to this myth is what made Disney so successful and why Las Vegas has tried to turn itself, with mixed results, into a family destination center. But as usual, hot button marketers must market to the dream; consumers want to close their eyes to the reality. It's the dream of the nuclear family sharing family dinners rather than vying for time in front of the TV or the computer. In the fifties and sixties, television actually served to bring people together. As most households had only one television, families watched it together. Moreover, unlike the dizzying array of channels and hundreds of programs available today via cable, there were only a handful of programs on the air. Watching television, at least decades ago, was quality time for the family.

the american work ethic has changed things

Fulfillment of desires often involves acquiring services and products. Products and services cost money. Thus, average American parents are so busy working to pay for everything that they often can't find the time they need to be with their kids. A *Newsweek* study showed that people are so busy that they neglect the things that are important to them. Husbands and wives say they don't even have the time or inclination to make love as often as they once did. Interestingly, other cultures, particularly Hispanics, are more closely bonded in the nuclear family. The family dinner still rules in their culture. Hasidic Jews make it a point to spend Friday nights together to pray or to reinforce family moments.

For many families, on the other hand, the car is the new gathering place. Believe it or not, the average American spends more time communicating with his or her kids and spouse in the car rather than in the home. The average driver now spends the equivalent of nearly a full month each year stuck in traffic or shepherding the kids to work and play. So, as we'll see in the Poverty of Time Hot Button, manufacturers have created portable foods that the family can eat in the car. Marketers have created games that the family can play in the car. Some marketers have even developed DVD players so the kids can watch movies in the car. The family car is a major avenue for market development.

the aspirational family

Family is the emotional heart of most people's lives. According to a study done in Canada, most family values are still highly traditional. The study pointed out that the ideal traditional family is just that—an ideal. Family values are like standards of quality. We will never reach them 100 percent of the time. But people will always strive for them. That's the key thing marketers need to know. Most people grow up and aspire to marry, have children who are happy and healthy, and to be good parents. The same ideas that were important at the turn of the nineteenth century are as important in the twenty-first century.

The study pointed out that 90 percent of teens desire to get married, raise children, and stay with their partners for the rest of their lives. The study showed very high levels of agreement regarding the importance of children learning such values as honesty, personal responsibility, getting along with others, politeness, reliability, and concern for others.

family values are key to selling houses

Real estate agents still suggest that house sellers bake cookies in their ovens when a potential buyer comes over for a viewing. The aroma helps conjure the myth of a family at home together baking. As in everything, salespeople and hot button marketers must market to aspirations—in this case, the myth of a family all in the same place at the same time. Consumers very much want to be like the myth. While today's mom is not up early in her housedress—now she's putting on makeup and catching her train to the office—she wants to know that she is raising a family with the values that she and her spouse agree upon. This is why smart marketers created something called meal solutions. Michelangelo's Italian Foods, Nancy's Natural Foods, and Chef America are just some of the companies that have put dinners on the table that require minimal preparation.

One focus group participant defined a meal solution as a meal you don't have to cook yourself, but that tastes like you did. It gives Mom a way to manage and maintain her concept of family values—even though her routine or lifestyle may bear no resemblance to the June Cleaver picture to which she aspires.

In fact, most women today say that they can't come close to cooking like their mothers did. But did their mothers make everything from scratch? Hell no. The previous generation had microwaves, prepared dinners like Hamburger Helper, boxed cake mixes and mashed potatoes, and most of the same luxuries of this post-boomer generation. Again, aspirations and ideals have created the myth.

Variety, speed of preparation, and cleanup time are the buzzwords for family food marketers. But hot button marketers must remember one thing: You can't substitute convenience for quality. Consumers simply won't pay for it. Family values has much to do with valuing the family itself—consumers won't want to give their family something they feel is poor tasting or less nutritious.

marketing insight

Americans are staying home more. According to an International Housewares Association news release, Americans are seeking the safety and comfort of home. There's also an increase in home-based activities such as scrapbooking, gardening, knitting, jewelry making, and other crafts as well as leisure cooking, says A. J. Riedel, senior partner of Riedel Marketing Group.

dad is still a big influence in car sales

The evolution in the marketing of SUVs makes for a fascinating case history about family values. They were originally sold on the Control Hot Button. "You can master all of the elements in your new SUV." Then, in addition to mastering the elements, they were promoted as a replacement station wagon. "Pack your team and get ready to go." Then the media published crash tests that showed SUVs were clear-cut winners in collisions with standard-sized cars. So the pitch was (subconsciously), protect your family with the heavily armored SUV. The message works so well that one new father shopping for cars commented that he had to buy an SUV as a defensive measure because everyone else on the road had SUVs—one example of family values marketing run wild.

However, Mom, Dad, and the kids are more than components of the larger whole (i.e., the family). They are individuals. While in marketing the family can be considered a unit, the target should be the individual. In the traditional family, there can be Mom, Dad, and each kid. But while families strive to be traditional, for the most part, many families are unique. Teens are their own subspecies, and for all the heavy metal, rap music, and rebellion, they tend to derive their values from their families and defer to them in most ways. Left to their own devices, they buy the same toothpaste, food, and other products important to their health that Mom would approve of.

But they still want to make their own statement. For this they use store-bought symbols. These symbols include clothes, piercings, music players, cars, candy, and other products that show their independence from Mom and Dad.

the kid kwotient

To paraphrase F. Scott Fitzgerald (who said it about the rich), kids aren't like you and me. They're irrational, impulsive, compulsive, and generally feel that the Earth spins on an axis that has them at the center. Come to think of it, kids *are* a lot like you and me. Children affect over 60 percent of the family's market purchases. The trick is to find out which 60 percent they do impact and in what ways they influence the purchase decision. It varies from category to category. The nice thing about kids is that they are a self-replenishing resource. According to licensors of kids' products, the generational cycle is eight years, from about four to twelve years of age. That means that every eight years, there's a new market for kids' toys.

As Disney knows, kids haven't changed much over the years. They're more informed because of the grip of mass media, but the same motivations that grabbed kids years ago still work today. The urge to party, to be popular, to stand out in the crowd, and to not stand out in the crowd are all driving forces. Don't show a child in a solitary setting. Kids are social beings and when you show a kid all alone in a commercial, no matter how cute he may look to you, it makes your product (and the user) look like an outcast.

Do show a kid older than your target audience. Kids look up to older kids. They easily identify with them. To be like the big boys is an essential kidlike desire. It's anathema to show kids

marketing insight Despite how busy women's lives are today many of them still take a great deal of pride in keeping and maintaining a neat, well-maintained home (which goes to the Control and Nurturing Hot Buttons). A great deal of their identity stems from this family role. However, there is a great deal of difference between the working mom and the "professional homemaker" (who doesn't work outside the home) in the way you need to reach them. Working women want efficiency, speed, and convenience in the products and services they buy to care for the home. The "professional homemaker" responds to power and uniqueness.

younger than your target group. It makes your product look "babyish" and unsophisticated to your target audience.

Most kids instinctively know how far they can expect their mom to bend. Don't think getting past the gatekeeper is simple. No way. The dynamics change according to what parenting stage the parent is going through, the age of the child, and the order of the children's birth.

the trend is for ready-made, packaged fun

With Mom and Dad hopping around trying to make a living, it can become hard to entertain kids. That's why hot button marketers are offering prepackaged fun. Birthday parties for the younger set are as apt to take place at a fun center in a local mall, with a concept like Fun Craft. Mom brings the kids. The company supplies, literally, Fun-in-a-Box. Samantha Feig, manager of one of the stores, says, "Fun Craft specializes in encouraging creativity and physical activity in one party. Parties are an hour and a half long. For the first forty-five minutes, the children do a craft. The crafts range from plaster molds that the children paint, T-shirts that they draw on with fabric

marketing insight Don't forget Mom's role as the gatekeeper. Although there is a trend in our society for parents to involve their kids in marketplace decisions at earlier and earlier ages, children expect Mom to make the key purchase decisions on "serious" products, like nutritional foods, soaps, and health care products. Moms and their kids interact a great deal in the marketplace. Their interactions are usually positive and supportive. The challenge is to flavor their interactions in a way that is favorable to your product, such as putting cartoons on a frozen-dinner package. Mom gets health. Kids get play value—and perhaps get to eat with their fingers.

markers, paper puppets, to picture frames they can decorate, and so much more. The hostess helps the kids and gives them some creative advice. Once they are finished with the craft, we then go into the disco room. One of the girl DJs basically controls the party. She has to decide what games and dances to play and also leads the kids in the dances." Mom usually books the party and both parents pay the bill.

Here's how to do it right—as presented in a real TV commercial: A man and a boy are going to a baseball game. The camera shows the boy's expressive face, and then the boy pounding his glove. Voice-over: "Two tickets to the season opener: eighty-eight dollars and fifty cents. Two programs, a hat, and a glove: sixty-five dollars and ninety-eight cents." The boy lunges at a ball that comes his way. Voice-over: "His first fly ball: priceless." The tag line scrolls across the TV and the voice reads aloud: "There are some things money can't buy. For everything else, there's MasterCard." A commodity credit card promoting family values? Priceless marketing.

pushing the hot button

for marketers
- If you're a family retailer, create mini "kids theme places" or "activity centers."
- Turn adult products into family products. America Online saw sales skyrocket when they introduced special sections for kids.
- Get involved with "family-oriented ratings" for various types of media.

for salespeople

- Stress the family concept in your sales pitch. For instance, if you're selling cars, stress how they can be used for safety reasons and actually be a key part of family outings.

- Expand your sell to the whole family. Get everyone involved. Suggest that kids (of the appropriate age) be at the meeting. For example, smoking cessation programs sometimes include kids at introductory meetings because research has shown that kids are the biggest motivators to get parents to stop smoking.

- Make the whole family part of the purchase decision. Stress the need to get family consent on appropriate products.

- Use sales materials that appeal to kids. Kids love getting and playing with "adult items" like carpet swatches and tiles.

- Keep a list of birthdays. Almost anyone will tell you theirs. Send cards or make a phone call at the proper time. Almost everyone feels special on their birthday and they will get the warm fuzzies when you treat them as a person and not as a client. (This "push" can apply to other hot buttons too.)

chapter 10
the desire to belong

what marketers need to know

The need to belong is a particularly important hot button for marketers and salespeople to understand. People are social animals. They want and need to connect with others who are like themselves, share the same interests, and have the same needs. They look to others for validation and they buy from people they like and trust. When they buy, they look for and buy the products and the specific brands that others in their identity groups buy.

how marketers can apply this

In order to get the most bang for your buck when it comes to marketing to the Desire to Belong Hot Button, you, as a hot button marketer or salesperson, must feed the customer's need for emotional connections. Many people look to fulfill their emotional need to belong via membership in groups. Smart marketers and salespeople embrace groups, clubs, and associations as a powerful marketing tool. They learn what their members want and what their frame of reference is for purchasing decisions. Groups give marketers the ammunition they need to make the sales. All you need to do is match your products and services to the needs, interests, and values of members of each group.

tools that appeal to the need to belong
Colors and Color Combinations
Decals
Logos
Mascots
Slogans
Titles
Ph.D., ScD, R.N., M.D., and other designations
Clothes
Code words
Tools

create affinity groups

Super hot button marketers and salespeople will actually take the Desire to Belong Hot Button to entirely new levels. Because they know how strong the need for belonging is, savvy marketers should look for opportunities to create new social and affinity groups when appropriate. Even if there's already a similar group, there's always room for another one—a Saturday Morning Toastmasters group (if there's one in your area, make it a Sunday Afternoon Toastmasters), a Monday evening softball league, an archery team just for people who are sixty-plus. It doesn't matter how many similar groups there are. Like the old Jell-O ads said, "There's always room for more." There's even a new magazine called *Geezer Jocks* published by people who realize that there is a targeted grouping of older people who like to be competitive and engage in sports.

Paradoxically, groups are transient in nature. They come and go. Their boundaries are fluid and members move freely between them, and their boundaries frequently interconnect. So it's important to be aware of similarities and diversities as you move between them.

belonging—what's it all about?

Humans are social beings. They bond with their families, friends, groupings of people, and institutions for many reasons. Sometimes this bonding is the basis for survival—certainly it was critical for survival for our ancestors. But there's a lot more to the need to belong than that. We all long to be accepted. This need to belong is all wrapped up in our sense of personal and psychological well-being—our sense of personal worth.

Belonging doesn't just happen. Belonging is based on shared perceptions, imitation, and mirroring. Understanding how belonging works is key to a hot button marketer's success. Hot button marketers recognize the signals and evidence of belonging and use them effectively.

For example, we know that all humans smile. Smiling, as adults, is a learned behavior we use to tell each other we have something in common—to signal to the other person that we're alike more than we're different. Smiling says "I'm okay—you're okay." But, what we smile about varies from culture to culture and from group to group. There are many other evidences and accoutrements that say "I belong."

Americans, as a general group, are the joiningest people in the world. The proof is probably in your wallet. How many clubs do you belong to? How many associations? Check your wallet for starters. Do you have a Gold Card or a Platinum Card? Do you have a voter's card? Do you own clothing that has the logo of your high school or college alma mater?

So, for example, if you are a scuba diver, you will feel an immediate bond with anyone displaying a Scuba Association logo. You may buy a scuba watch. A waterproof watch is critical even if it won't keep time more accurately than any other watch, but more than that, it's a waterproof watch that maybe includes a compass and a depth monitor and a Scuba Association logo . . . well, who could doubt what your interests are then? You may also wear a T-shirt that broadcasts the location of your last dive or one that reads: "I'm a scuba diver." And, you may even display a bumper sticker that reads: "Scuba. Do you?" People want to be among people who are like themselves. They use accoutrements to broadcast their identities and attract others like themselves.

Coffee drinkers are another excellent example. Coffee fanatics want to show that they know and enjoy real coffee. They display unroasted coffee beans in their kitchens to show that they are part of an elite group. Perhaps no one really cares whether a person will go to the trouble of roasting and grinding their own beans, but it makes the user feel special—and others who share this passion recognize it as a basis of belonging to a group. Of course, many coffee consumers are also joining coffee associations, like *www.betterbeans.com* and a variety of coffee-of-the-month clubs.

groups . . . groups everywhere

People join groups because they want to belong. They like to know that there are lots of other people out there like them who enjoy the same things and buy the same products. They rely on their groups for validation and respect. In America, there is a group for everyone, including those who own yellow Mustangs (the car, not the horse)—Yellow Mustang Registry, at *www.yellowmustangregistry.com*. All are legitimate sales outlets, or you can utilize them for market research and information—and save yourself the expense of false leads or inappropriate marketing and sales approaches. Most groups fall into the following categories.

aspirational

The aspirational reference group consists primarily of other people or groups that consumers would most like to resemble or be compared with. Many businesses use athletes to get their message across. In fact, in one study in Houston, more people would rather hear or meet baseball pitcher and Houstonian Roger Clemens than George W. Bush or his dad. The closer a person is—or was—to achieving his dream, the easier it is to market him or her. No, we can't be Roger Clemens, but we can wear his

---

marketing insight   Salespeople/marketers sell best when they sell to people like themselves. This is where social groups are so important. You need to be proactive in any social event in which you participate. Smart hot button marketers know how to capitalize on the social and affinity groups that they already belong to. Take a few minutes to consider all the various groups you belong to. Do you go to church? Play in a bowling league? Play racquetball? Are you a hunter? An airline pilot? Do you participate in political activities? Each group is a superb base for getting acquainted with people that you know and understand because you have something in common with them. Groups give marketers the ammo to make the sales. All you need to do is match your products and services to the needs and interests of members of each group.

jersey with his name or number. Obviously, if you didn't play baseball as a kid and dream, for at least a moment, of being a big leaguer or a celebrity, you won't be a member of this particular aspirational group.

social

This is probably the most important of all groups. People want to belong to groups of people that are "just like me." One book club specifically suggests in its advertising that its members are "a breed apart" from conventional readers of popular books. In fact, as was mentioned in Chapter 7, once a book, movie, or TV show becomes mainstream, many people won't buy it. Social groups are the reason for the success of many products such as Tupperware and Mary Kay Cosmetics. Many people, particularly women, go for the social aspects of the "show and sell" approach. Peer cajoling adds subtle pressure to buy something, but that's not nearly as important as the woman's ability to enjoy the social bonding that these groups offer. Interestingly, the male consumer has never been a target for such marketing—even though it seems to make sense to sell power tools and other manly things in the party context. While male consumers don't particularly like the party context, they do join other social groupings and associations, like the Rotary, Freemasons, and clubs related to their profession or industry.

commonality

Commonality groups include people who represent the consumer's equals. They can be coworkers, neighbors, or members of religious groups, or special-interest groups or organizations. The banking community has marketed credit cards this way for years. You name it and you can get a credit card that ties you to a particular group. Lance Armstrong and others who picked up on the trend have sold more than 50 million "LiveStrong" bracelets to benefit cancer patients, survivors, and research. Wearing the bracelets says to other wearers "I, too, have been touched by cancer and I care about what you care about."

groups are the ultimate world wide web

Hot button marketers understand that groups are intertwined. For each group there are countless offshoots and variants. Each of these groups and subgroups speaks its own language and establishes its own standards of acceptable behavior. Take, for example, Americans as a group or a collective. Hot button marketers know that you don't approach, market, or sell to Native Americans the same way as you would Latin Americans, or African Americans, or Caucasians. You don't market to people in the Bronx in the same way you would to consumers on the North Shore of Chicago, or in Phoenix. And you don't talk to farmers in Nebraska like you talk to people in Boston. First-generation immigrants have very different needs and

marketing insight Consumers use groups, or more aptly, affinities, to define their place in the sun, for informational purposes, and to separate themselves from others. Members of clubs also serve the role of surrogate friends. Many people play team sports for the fun of the sport. But they also desire to belong. At a series of focus groups, people who played team sports were asked why. Did they play for the camaraderie or for winning? Would they rather be on a winning team of gung-ho personalities who go separate ways after the game or a losing team that gathers together after the game for good times? Most of the people chose the latter. Camaraderie beat winning hands down.

perceptions from second-generation immigrants. Smart hot button marketers pay particular attention to those nuances.

people bond through groups and affinities
People link up with each other in many ways. Sometimes geography brings people together in a neighborhood. In these cases the bonding may be forced on us through neighborhood organizations and "clubs" we "must" join if we want to buy a house or live in a certain neighborhood. Sometimes we come together through our own choice of organizations. Sometimes the groups we belong to appeal to us through birth or shared history or interests. Communities or groups create bonds and boundaries for both insiders and outsiders.

The sports section of a major newspaper did a "Where Are They Now" article about what retired athletes missed most about the games they used to play. Surprisingly, they didn't talk about the home runs they hit, the exorbitant salaries they made, or the applause and cheers of the crowd. They almost unanimously said, "The guys in the locker room." The important part of the athletes' lives most often came before and after the final out was made. The players were among people like themselves. They belonged.

Going a little bit further with the analogy, the desire to belong is also the reason for the upsurge in licensed athletic wear. People are showing their loyalty and affinity to the people wearing the same gear and declaring the same loyalties.

like breeds like
The strongest affinity association is based on age. Whenever there are groups of people at a party, or an event, individuals

will gravitate toward other people of the same age. Entire markets are built on this truth. Florida and Sun City, Arizona, for example, grew into highly desirable retirement areas—why? Because aging Chicagoans and New Yorkers encouraged members of their groups back home to come join them.

As one example, Campbell Taggart, a bread manufacturer, created a highly successful club for kids based on their IronKids Bread. The product was white bread that promised all the nourishment of whole wheat—and it was marketed to kids. The campaign was incredibly effective. The name IronKids created an affinity with kids who wanted to be strong and muscular, and to moms who wanted a nutritious white bread. Create a club for your product and base a product around it. It sounds backward (you usually create the product first), but it works. One imperative to remember when developing a group: You need to choose a group that people can aspire to. If you appeal to kids, always show kids older than your target market. If the identity you choose is inappropriate, too lame, or too far out there, your campaign will not succeed.

group dynamics in action

Consumers, as a rule, generally don't put up a lot of resistance to group pressure. In fact, most people actually welcome this kind of peer pressure because it gives them a frame of reference for the things they buy and use as well as assurance that they're making the right decision. Affinity groups provide vital information on how people should act and do things. In *Why They Buy*, by Robert B. Settle and Pamela L. Alreck, the authors list three ways that groups serve as comparisons and furnish guidelines for what we buy.

information groups

Formal and informal affinity groups provide data about the psychological, symbolic, and material attributes of a good or service. It shows the consumer what exists and what alternatives are available. Both Best Buy and Trader Joe's create affinity groups and/or send out informative newsletters about their products that are geared to these groups (electronics and gourmet food, respectively).

Today, when consumers connect to the Internet and join a group, there is usually a section where the customer can ask for a newsletter or guidance about a particular purchase. Some of the more advanced Web sites have forums where people can post information and provide help about a particular product or purchase. If you're looking for a new game, you have the option of logging onto a game site and asking questions about whether a game has play value or is worth the time and money that you're going to put into it. Also, good salespeople, marketers, and Internet sites ask for tons of information about you so they can determine who you use as your reference group. The American Dental Association is a reference group for people who need work on their teeth. The American Marketing Association, similarly, serves up useful information for marketers.

comparative groups

This group sets the social and benchmark standards. Play sports? Then you have to wear Nikes. Comparative groups are usually about status and how to achieve it in others' eyes. It can be very difficult for consumers to gauge their status within a group. When that happens, they turn to their comparative group for guidelines. The group provides a standard or sets the stage for the unwritten code governing what is cool or acceptable—hot button marketers learn the code and work within the social and benchmark standards of the customers to whom they're trying to market.

Benchmarking is frequently used in technology circles, such as in hospital organizations and in business. Most investors use "the Dow," while equity mutual funds and portfolio managers use the S&P 500 Index as the benchmark to beat.

normative or peer groups

Each group establishes norms and unwritten behaviors within the group and outside the group. These tell the members what to do and what not to do in social situations. In the normative group, members influence what is perceived to be "right," "proper," "responsible," or "cool." Understanding these perceptions is most important to hot button marketers. We see this

---

real-life example   Years ago, there was a beer brewery in New York that created an advertising campaign showing how various ethnic groups consumed their beer. The campaign won a great many awards. The ads showed Jewish people, Greeks, and other ethnic groups drinking beer in fun environments like weddings and confirmations. It was meant to show a celebratory experience.

The company then created a commercial using Hispanics as their ethnic category. At this time, Hispanics had a bad reputation among biased African Americans and Caucasians because many of the immigrants lived in poverty and didn't have much formal education. New York Hispanics were new immigrants from Puerto Rico and faced the same hurdles that most new ethnic groups faced when they first came to the United States, including extreme prejudice. Rival beer companies showed beer retailers the commercial and slyly pointed out that their customers would resent being lumped into a social grouping with Puerto Ricans. Sales dropped dramatically and the beer company never truly recovered. That's why it's imperative to research the groups you're going to use in your ads.

in practice at the workplace. For example, if you work for Jose Cuervo, a major maker of Tequila, you don't ask for a Margarita. You must have a Cuervo Margarita. If you work for Coca-Cola, you never ever go to Pizza Hut, which is owned by archrival PepsiCo. These behaviors, which start out as informal "guidelines," quickly become ingrained due to peer pressure and the group dynamics of belonging. A member of a religious group may even wear a symbol of that group outside his or her house of worship, because the religion is a part of the person's identity.

To summarize, groups are sales fodder for marketers and salespeople. They are often linked by common interests, shared experiences, and desires. Hot button marketers understand that groups are intertwined. For each group there are countless offshoots and variants. Each of these groups and subgroups speaks its own language and establishes its own standards of acceptable behavior. When you understand the language, behavior, and similarities of a particular group, you can begin to make strong inroads to sales success.

pushing the hot button

for marketers
- In retail stores, create a sale or affiliation for people who have bought similar products. Supermarkets collect this information from discount scanning cards they hand out to their customers.
- Create logos, key chains, and other identifiers that signify belonging to a certain club or group.
- Create products that meet the special needs of a particular age group.

- Develop a concept or even a store that a certain, targetable group would like to rebel against or, at the very least, not like to be associated with. The Gap name capitalizes on the generational gap between teens and parents.
- When using celebrities or role models in your marketing to a specific group, find celebrities who are truly representative of the group members. Elizabeth Taylor wouldn't be a good choice for marketing cleaning supplies to housewives. Martha Stewart might be.

for salespeople

- On the Internet, "social circle" data is now being collected and stored in databases (like Friendster, Ryze, and many, many other Web sites). Search this data. Peer-based marketing is highly effective in targeting prospects.
- Use the names of famous people who use your product. Michael Jordan took his place as a marketing icon because of the aspirational nature of his sporting appeal. Also use the names of neighborhood people or those who belong to a similar club or social unit.
- Put your product on TV or in the movies. The mere association of goods and services with a storyline and its characters provides a strong reference group appeal.
- Start your own club that appeals to your target audience. For instance, if you teach computers, start a computer club for people who see themselves as novices.

chapter 11

fun is its own reward

what marketers need to know

Life is short. Meetings are dull. Selling is stressful. None of these alleged truisms have to be true at all when you add fun and games to the marketing mix. It's not hard. Just get in touch with your inner child and spread this good humor to your prospects. Introduce them to activities that are fun and enjoyable. People buy from people they like, and humor greases the wheel for sales. Add a bit of fun into the lives of your prospects and they will often lose their skepticism. Adding a bit of humor often builds trust and makes you more convincing.

how marketers can apply this

People often choose venders because they can have fun with them. Yes, it's true. After making an hour-long pitch to a bunch of corporate types, I asked them what they looked for in choosing a vendor, all things being equal. They said they wanted to have a good time on the road. There I was, pouring out my heart and soul to a prospect, playing up all of my qualifications and the benefits of the product and services I could offer, and they wanted a guy who knew where all the hot clubs in Chicago were. I now know where they were coming from. Any product and service will receive more attention and sales if you appeal to your customer's fun-loving side.

let's get serious here

Now we're going to have a serious discussion about fun and humor. Sound like a contradiction in terms? It's not. Fun is serious business, and it's a hard sell to classically trained management. But it's an important hot button because fun, stimulation, and laughter are part of every culture. We all don't laugh at the same things, but we all have a desire to laugh and to be stimulated. So what is so important about fun? After all, these are serious times. It's important because everyone has a need to be stimulated. Fun is a great common denominator. You can use humor every day to ease stressful relationships. After all, what can be more stressful than selling to people every day (people who, most likely, have seen some version of your product or service from about ten different competitors)? Of course, if you read and apply the tools in this book, there should be little stress. However, fun is another tool you can have in your arsenal. Fun is a great motivator and a great problem solver on many levels.

For instance, if you sell washing machines, how can you tell your consumers that your washing machine is better than others? You could offer a guarantee, but how does the consumer know you're going to back it up? *Everyone* has guarantees. Maytag, a famous washing machine maker, broke the mold and created an advertising campaign that brought it to the top of its class.

The commercials featured a paunchy guy, dressed in repairman's clothes. He gives a speech to his repairman staff. He warns them that they are going to be the loneliest men in the world. In later commercials, he sits around feeling sorry for himself and tries little tricks to keep himself busy. He checks out the phone to see if it's working. He says in mocking self-pity, "I'm the loneliest guy in the world." It became a national buzz phrase. We laughed with him, not at him, because we were in on the joke. He's the Maytag repair guy and never gets calls because Maytags don't break down. And if they did, our sweet lovable Maytag repairman would be thrilled to fix them.

This "Loneliest Guy in the World" commercial helped sell more washing machines than any other brand. The lonely Maytag Repairman was a strong character with a well-defined personality. He stood as the symbol of dependability for more than twenty-five years, helping to identify Maytag as "the dependability people."

When Maytag based its campaign on fun, it paid close attention to an essential ingredient of fun—they changed the commercial often. They made sure to keep viewers stimulated with new situations. The ads were fun, and the Lonely Maytag Man became a mnemonic for reliability.

If you're going to run a humorous commercial or ad, change it often. Punch lines become stale quickly.

companies can use humor to sell "serious products"

Ever run an ad that told the world that your car was a lemon? A sly German company tried that. The ads said the car was homely. It would not go as fast as other cars on the road. It didn't even have a radiator! Volkswagen broke all the rules with those ads, but their self-deprecation was fun to watch. And, it introduced the Volkswagen brand to America. Americans identified with the homeliness of the cars.

Fast-forward to today. Best Buy introduces the Geek Squad. Best Buy knew, perhaps better than most of their competitors, that for many people who have computers, fixing them is a serious issue. Enter the tongue-in-cheek Geek Squad. Best Buy's Geek Squad employs white-shirted men and women with skinny, out-of-date snap-on ties (a.k.a., Geek wear). Their mission, for a fee, is to convert consumer wrath about complicated gadgets into warm and fuzzy feelings. They even drive up in geeky black Volkswagen bugs. Now, that's a fun treatment for a serious problem. The Geek Squad even sells $129 house-call gift cards specifically for setting up digital camera equipment and software.

Many top advertisers, marketers, and salespeople argue that marketing is serious business and that they, and their customers, don't have the dollars to waste on frivolity. Word to the wise: Lighten up! Don't take yourself and your product so seriously. You can have fun with your product—and make money. Almost any product can be fun if you appeal to the child in the consumer. Fun is not just for kids anymore. Take, for example, Brookstone, the famous catalogue merchant, which just devoted an entire Christmas catalog to toys for adults. Electronic stores actually take great pains to make sure that people play with their products. They realize that fun is a primary hot button.

fun is the sugar coating on life

Fun makes unpalatable things palatable. Fun can disarm the prospect because it lessens the tension of the sale. It makes the salesperson and the product itself more likeable. People buy from people they like. Fun caters to our innate want of stimulation.

Look at the Chia pet. Originally it was a cheesy-looking clay animal filled with grass seeds. No big deal there. Except that people liked watching the inanimate object grow "fur." Now you can buy a whole line of Chia pets. If you were going to sell miniature brine shrimp that would die in a week or so, not a whole lot of people would be interested. But call them Sea Monkeys and you have a product that's been selling for more than twenty years.

The whole reason for adding fun to a product is to enhance the buyer's perception of pleasure and to satisfy his or her need to be stimulated. That's really not as difficult as it sounds. It can be as simple as adding a scent, a new taste, or a new texture. Make it grow bigger when you add water. The more senses you can get involved in a product, the more emotionally involved a consumer gets. Even riding an exercise bike can be fun when you add a computer game or allow the consumer to check his or her progress in order to develop a "personal best."

fun is a break from the day-to-day business of living

There's a reason why newspapers, except the *New York Times*, offer comic strips. People like to laugh. In fact, when a newspaper dumps an old, favorite comic strip, they are as swamped with as many complaints as if they dumped their daily crossword.

Crossword puzzles are also fun and a prime driver of newspaper sales.

Bulletin boards at most places of businesses are peppered with cartoons. Dilbert, the ultimate corporate misfit, has become an icon for many people because it allows people to laugh at the very truths of the business world. Actually, Dilbert might be considered blasphemous in some business-oriented cultures, but here we place our problems into the Dilbert cartoon, and it somehow salves our anger.

marketing insight

Don't sacrifice your product's benefits with frivolity. Although humor can draw your customer in, you have to be very careful about how you use it. One company created a line of Dilbert mints. The product failed. Why? The joke was stronger than the product. Although the presentation was funny, Dilbert didn't suggest a good-tasting breath mint. The imagery was inconsistent and the association flawed.

boredom is a negative hot button

One of the negative hot buttons is fear of boredom. People want to be stimulated. Prospects find stimulation in the presence of unexpected pleasure. They want to be knocked off their ennui.

Fun is curiosity. Fun is trying a product you never tried before just to see what happens. It is also the cure for the "running in place" syndrome. Most people are mired in habitual living. They do their chores, go to work, and keep on running just to keep up the status quo. Novelty dispels the tedium. Novelty is stimulation. It breaks through the clutter of the hundreds of marketing pitches that people see and hear all day long.

The Energizer Bunny ads work because they break through the seriousness of daily life. Batteries aren't fun to buy. But if we remember the Bunny, it might lighten up a dull purchase. Keep in mind, though, the humor has to be applicable to the product being marketed, as with the Energizer Bunny ads. Most commercials that use humor alone don't work.

fun can be alchemy

People like the addition of magic to their lives. As a marketer or salesperson, you can supply that magic. Fun is mixing ingredients to make bread. Who (excusing professional bakers) has not been stimulated by dough, somehow magically rising? And, do you remember how Jell-O used to be fun? You just add hot water, let it cool, and you have a dessert. Add some fruits and a mold and you have something special. There's magic in products that change color or effervesce. What is carbonated water (seltzer), after all? It's plain water that plays games on your tongue. Fun can also be a unique label on a wine. Wine producers are now discovering that for the first time buyers can be stimulated into action with a unique label.

fun is important in business-to-business scenarios, too

Almost all professional motivators use humor in their acts. Humor helps break through the dullness and numbers that people expect from business presentations. Companies often choose a supplier because he or she seems like "one of us"—they can have a good time with the person after work. Why does this matter? As I mentioned, having a good time with a client helps businesspeople bond together. It helps build relationships.

fun doesn't have to make you laugh

Novelty is the fuel of creativity and innovation. We are programmed to create and change and to seek relief from the mundane. Repeating the same action time after time can be deadly dull. The vice president of one of the largest compilers of marketing information says that one of the biggest issues on the job is how people can have more fun. That means you can add fun to business-to-business products. Lighten up on your next PowerPoint presentation and stimulate your audience.

how to use fun and humor

Make sure the humor relates to the point you are making. The point of humor and novelty is not to generate laughter—although it helps if people are in on the joke. The point is to make a point—to suggest some aspects of your product or market, and to lead the consumer gently to a buying decision. The humor should tie in with some aspect of your product. This could be a delicate situation. A person with a serious medical condition doesn't want to be the butt of a joke. However, the doctors and nurses in charge of fixing the condition frequently use "gallows humor" to unwind and relax. This may be okay as an inside joke, but patients might find it horrific—even downright morbid. Timing and sensitivity are critical here. Be careful.

humor, fun, and novelty are catalysts

In technical terms, a catalyst is when two chemicals get together to form a chemical reaction and create something new. Humor or novelty can be used to get the salesperson and prospect to bond together. Humor and novelty react with your customer and pitch to be more than the sum of its parts. Humor and novelty open doors. A salesperson who can add fun to a presentation loosens up the customer. Humor, fun, or stimulation is the catalytic agent. Laughing at the same joke bonds the salesperson and customer. Humor, by its mere presence, serves to smooth the way to sales. It contributes a socializing touch. But you have to know your customer. Some people like things very, very serious.

Someone once said, "Humor makes the whole world akin." Use the Fun Hot Button every day in your sales pitches. It can help you ease through awkward situations, make people smile, and lift the spirits of all those around you. Fun is a way of strengthening relationships between two or more people. Remember, more deals are done on the golf course than in the boardroom.

the psychology of it all

In a presentation, the prospect may enjoy the story but not care about the point—or the product. If you don't tie your humor to what you're trying to sell, the potential buyer may actively resent it. I met a salesperson who insisted on doing magic tricks as part of his sales pitches. I was fascinated and learned many new tricks. But a person who knew him well said he couldn't sell a thing even though he was so darned entertaining. He became a "Professional Visitor." People always said yes to his presentations but no to what he was selling. Humor, stimulation, and novelty must come from the heart. They cannot be acts or put-ons. The psychological function of humor and stimulation is simply to get the buyer's attention. And, to be successful, it must be totally related to the product.

When IBM introduced the PC, it used a person who looked like Charlie Chaplin. IBM chose the Chaplin character for a reason. He was actually a little less than Everyman—he was a dunce, but with a good heart. The Chaplin image broke through the clutter and made a point. People felt that if Charlie had a need for, and was able to use, a sophisticated machine, then so could they.

Just one more example: There is a new sunflower seed on the market called "Spitz." Most people would agree that spitting out sunflower seeds is not a particularly sexy thing to do. But that's what we do when we eat sunflower seeds. Humor is reality.

What some of your consumers may find funny, others might think is a complete turnoff. Rehearse your ad-libs. Research your commercials. If people laugh, that's fine. But, when push comes to shove, it's a lot better if people buy your product. Fun, novelty, and stimulation are conduits to the sale, not the be-all and end-all.

pushing the hot button

for marketers

- Create a Web site e-game around your product. When people play the game it reinforces the brand name and creates a fun image for your product. According to the *Washington Post,* Advergames can reinforce a brand image, build a database of information about its users, directly target a market to hit—all very inexpensively when compared to what it costs to advertise in other media.
- Give your product a funny name, like Mad Dog's Inferno Hot Sauce. The humor comes off like a breath of fresh air on the supermarket shelf. Lighten up your message.
- Change the color of your product to one that wouldn't be expected. Heinz had a decent run with its green ketchup.

Try a "scratch and sniff" label. It not only adds an element of sensory participation, but it gets your product into the prospect's hands.

- Have fun breaking conventional wisdom. Airline travel is supposed to be serious, but Southwest Airlines has taken to delivering the mandatory rules in funny, offbeat ways. It smoothes the ride and helps make Southwest stand out from the crowd.

- Create a fun demonstration. Most people still remember the construction worker in a hard hat stuck to a beam, supported only by Crazy Glue.

for salespeople

- Drop humorous stories into your pitch.
- Have fun at trade shows. Let participants play games and enjoy themselves. They will remember you and be a lot more receptive to return calls.
- Go to offbeat places for lunch meetings. Your buyers will remember the experience and see you in a better light than if you took them to a stuffy restaurant.
- Send humorous articles and e-mails to prospects. It helps build a cordial relationship.

chapter 12

poverty of time

what marketers need to know

You might wonder why these chapter summaries are coming at the beginning of the chapter instead of the end as in many other books. My esteemed editor said our readers want the key information fast. Thus, we made this small change to save you time, because to most people, time is of the essence. Consumers have more time, but they tend to use all the time they have. It's a distinctly American characteristic. Other industrialized countries give their workers more time off, more holiday paid leave, and more time—for both moms and dads—to be with their families. For us? We try to squeeze more activities into the time we have. Most consumers don't have time to smell the roses, unless they purchased them in a store. After all, they take too damn long to cultivate and grow.

how marketers can apply this

Time is the new coin of the realm. Hot button marketers understand that the issue is not time but simply that, overall, people don't know how to use the time they have. What, as a hot button marketer or salesperson, are you to do? Create solutions such as time management products and multitasking opportunities. Sixty percent of Super Bowl viewers last year were simultaneously playing on the Internet. Help people cram more into

155

their day. GEICO's ad campaign promises "If you have fifteen minutes, you can save a bundle on your car insurance." They don't even ask for a half-hour—just fifteen minutes. Play up convenience, but don't substitute quality. Shorten the learning curve of your products. Tighten up your sales pitch. Keep your advertising copy crisp and to the point.

i want it now—i don't have time to wait

The sundial started it all. It helped us keep track of time. And we've been trying to beat the clock ever since. Consumers, especially Americans, are looking to beat time so badly, they're almost in desperation mode. Walter Fox, a brand consumerist, calls it "tyranny of the urgent." Americans feel that they're in a gigantic time bind that they can't get out of. The time bind has made America an instant-gratification society. They want instant satiation in cooking, cleaning, eating, working, and just about every endeavor. In sporting events, people complain about how long the game takes, even if they enjoy this leisure activity. Consumers want to save time in almost everything they do. They seek to buy back precious minutes and this is manifested in the products they buy and the services they use. E-mails, airplanes, digital photography, quick-working therapies, and instant medicine are what drive consumers. Polaroid thought they had a lock on the American public with instant pictures. Consumers had to wait a whole minute to see a picture come to life. Now, with digital photography, consumers have to wait a whole second. And digital camera manufacturers are coupling with printer manufacturers to make it even faster. Hot button marketing at work!

how are consumers fighting the perceived paucity of time?

According to several studies, consumers actually have more free time today than they had thirty years ago. They are simply cramming more into every day. So, how do they spend their free time? Cooking, cleaning, eating, working, commuting—the same way their parents spent their free time. As in everything in this book, the paucity of time is based on consumer perception.

This whole "timeless" phenomenon has given us a new word. It's called "multi-tasking." People are buying books on disk so they can turn drive time—those hours we're sitting in traffic jams on the freeways—into productive time. Consumers complain about the time they spend at airports. Coming and going, they spend about four hours touring airports and looking for anything to make this time useful.

ten-minute meals, five-minute workouts: deliver quick fixes

Saving time is one of the biggest motivators for men and women ages twenty-five to forty-five. This is particularly true for women in their childbearing years and for those with young children. Despite the fact that society has become somewhat more progressive, taking care of the kids and putting dinner on the table is still largely considered the woman's job, and it takes time. Infants aren't going to wait. It doesn't matter if the woman works forty hours a week, attends PTA meetings in the evening, and is writing computer software in her spare time. For males, working harder and longer means less quality time with the kids, and often they have to try to fit in multiple families, due to the high divorce rate

americans choose working harder vs. playing harder

Customers depend on hot button marketers and inventors to come up with new ways to do things faster. Hot button marketers and inventors have done their part. American Express and Chase are developing innovative credit cards with a computer chip to make transactions faster and easier.

From the Magic Bullet Speed Blender to faster computers, much of the technology employed for the pursuit of progress has been to satisfy the Poverty of Time Hot Button. The ability to save time has always been the hallmark of industrial and supply and demand revolutions. Timesaving innovations have transformed patterns of production and consumption over the last 200 years. Inventors recognized that the ultimate product of the work they developed was more time for consumers to enjoy leisure activities. That was the intent, but it hasn't worked that way. In fact, the end result was just the opposite. Americans are cramming more activities into the time that these inventions actually save.

convenience means time management

What most marketers see as convenience products, hot button marketers see as time management tools. Most people don't have a lot of time to do what they have to do—let alone what they want to do. Many of us don't even sit down to eat our meals anymore.

Foods that can be considered car foods are a fast-growing category. A subset of these are called portable foods. A prerequisite for market entry is the food's ability to be consumed in a car, while driving. Research points out that a large percentage of meals are eaten while driving or riding in a car. Manufacturers are playing on consumers' needs for convenience, time efficiency, and tastiness—and, of course, multitasking. One marketer has even put macaroni and cheese in a push-up tube (similar to the ice cream that you enjoyed as a kid) to satisfy the need to save time.

The portable foods category, introduced by Chef America's Hot Pockets several years ago, has shown no signs of cooling down, with sales expected at $500 million this year. Campbell's has introduced Soup-to-Go. These products promise no muss, no fuss, and good taste. A microwave in a car for heating "portable car foods" might be an idea waiting to be discovered.

But saving someone time means more than just putting a dinner entrée in a frozen, microwavable rectangle. Your product has to perform as well—or even better—than products that don't save the customer hours of preparation. Take the case of bacon. It takes about thirty seconds for a strip of bacon to cook up in a microwave. But consumers wanted to save even more time. Tom Bush and Mark Schweiger, entrepreneurs and former brand mangers, created a product called Ready Crisp Fully Cooked Bacon for the microwave. These bacon strips cook up in a microwave in about five seconds. Many companies had failed some time back with the concept because saving twenty-five seconds was not a big deal. One obstacle they all encountered was that the precooked package was lighter than most uncooked bacon packages. It gave the false impression that consumers were not getting their money's worth. Schweiger and Bush solved the problem with tempting product photos on the package and a large "20 slices" descriptor. For reassurance, they put a clear window on the back, so people could see the quality of their product.

organization can mean saving time, too

The Day Runner, a time management system, jumped into the market lead with its "schedule-in-a-binder" paper system. People who thought themselves busy cherished the product. They felt it was just the thing they needed to juggle their work and professional lives. But the electronics manufacturers took it a step further by putting products that did the same thing as Day Runners into little computer-like gizmos called PDAs (for personal digital assistants), and they became the next time management toy.

Whether or not these organizers actually make a person more productive no one can say for sure. But businesspeople love to show off their fully scheduled PDA. Now these PDAs come with phone and e-mail capabilities—status seeking again (Hot Button #2—notice how motivations tie themselves together so nicely?) For some reason, people have a need to sort, categorize,

---

real-life example Years ago, a new airline started up. It featured a plethora of creature comforts—an open bar, entertainment, the works. The theory was to make travel fun, not exhausting. The catch . . . it took longer for people to get where they were going. The airline died. Despite all the luxuries, the customer simply wanted to get there fast.

and stow. It makes them feel that they're in control of their lives. It also helps them find things faster, If you have a product that organizes, the most effective way to show the benefit is with a simple, dramatic, before-and-after product shot on all of your sales material—and on the package in which it's presented.

time saving is an american thing

Many cultures say if you get there at this certain hour, okay, but they don't hold it against you if you don't. In Mexico, you should never violate their siesta, or resting time. This drives American businesspeople nuts. People's relationship to time even varies from state to state. In the northeastern states, the culture requires that you dart from one task to another. In the Southwest, it's another culture entirely. New Mexico is called the Land of Mañana. Very little gets done in the time frame specified. If a contractor or a plumber says he'll be there tomorrow, he might show up in a week—rarely apologizing. If you're a hot button marketer who is selling your product or service nationally, you need to be aware of regional distinctions.

doing what you want to do vs. what you have to do

Hot button marketers are careful to separate what the consumer chooses to do versus what the consumer has to do. I asked one person in a focus group what she does to make more time. She said she makes choices. America is the land of time choices. Hot button marketers can help consumers make those choices. Think about emotion and how much the consumer has vested in a task. No surprise here, but consumers usually procrastinate when it comes to things they really don't want to do. Humans are the only animals that can procrastinate. For instance, a cat won't look at a mouse and say, "I'll annoy it later." They do things as they come up. Consumers, on the other hand, will either put off a boring task or will multitask to get it out of the way. For instance, a dry cleaner opened up in a nearby train station. Since commuters don't particularly like the train ride or taking the clothes to the cleaner, they can kill both obnoxious birds at the same time.

Here is where "Feig's Correlation" comes in. A person will finish a certain task in the time psychologically allotted to it. If you sell a product that promises it will shine your windows in five minutes, then it had better do it. Five and a half minutes will be unacceptable, because we've allotted five minutes to it. Five-minute meals, ten-minute oil changes, faster car speeds are all products of the Poverty of Time Hot Button. All of these timesavers cost money (of course) so the consumer has to work even harder to make more money to pay for all of them—which leads to a greater lack of time. You know how it goes.

time is more of a problem for the upscale consumer

The more affluent a consumer is, the more possibilities and choices he/she has to make. The affluent may have many acquisitions, but they also tend to be poorest in time because they have to work harder to stay affluent and they have to spend more time buying and taking care of their possessions. Certain goods have to be researched, chosen, bought, set up, used, experienced, maintained, repaired, put away, and disposed of. And, some require a learning curve. All of these objects chew away at the consumer's time. We have more opportunities to lose time than ever before. This opportunity leads people to lose sight of their goals. I have been told by consumers, there are just too many choices (and the more money you earn the more choices you can indulge) in just about every category, including how to pay for the goods and services. Too many options can actually diminish enjoyment because of time demands.

Researchers also argue that Americans' sense of "time famine" stems from the increased emphasis on the "consumption" of experiences and from the phenomenon of "time deepening," doing more and doing things more quickly and simultaneously. Every ten years, there is a time study done by the American's Use of Time Project. Americans are asked to report their daily activities on an hour-by-hour basis. The results of these studies: people are highly inaccurate when estimating their own work time. Consumers have the time, but they consider their lives so frantic that they don't take the time to sort out things.

make your pitches fast and focused

Hot button marketers respond to consumers' poverty of time by making sure that their marketing efforts are tightly focused. They exercise their elevator messages (one-minute presentations) and they look for ways to engage their prospective

marketing insight   One of the more distasteful time killers for many people is the annual trip to the Motor Vehicle Bureau. One smart marketer opened five locations where consumers can register their cars, get their driver's license, and take care of typical bureaucratic operations. The trade-off is that it costs an extra $17.50 per transaction. However, business is booming. Americans simply don't want to wait for anything and they will pay dearly not to.

customers in the sales process in less-formal settings while they are doing something else—multitasking again? And, they are much more flexible. Hot button marketers are good multitaskers, too—able to shift on a dime to accommodate the short attention span of consumers who are starved for time. Hot button marketers know the consumer is going to pare down their sales pitch to one poignant sentence. Prospects don't have any more time than that. Hot button marketers know that customers will give a product in a store less than thirty seconds to connect or speak to them. Use your time wisely.

pushing the hot button

for marketers
- Make the time-saving aspects of your product real by showing the consumer or businessperson how much time they can free up for other, more pleasurable things.
- Try to solve two problems at once. Colgate Toothpaste with Mouthwash was made for those people who don't have time to use toothpaste and a mouthwash.
- Save the consumer as many steps as you can. Lipton Tea Bags allow consumers to brew iced tea without taking the time to boil water. General Mills Milk 'n Cereal Bars with cereal on the outside and milk filling inside eliminates

marketing insight   One group of consumer that is gaining time faster than the other groups is the revaluers (as described in Chapter 8). On average, the number of hours that baby boomers spend working is on the decline. Little surprise, with most of them heading into retirement. And they're using this surplus of time for their enjoyment. Another possible marketing avenue?

the step of pouring the cereal into a bowl and then add-ing milk. No spoons or bowls to wash either.

for salespeople

- Take your time at the beginning of a project to make sure you know what is exactly wanted. Scope out the project, identifying what is to be changed. Send a brief e-mail restating what has been said. Clients hate having to take the time to repeat their needs.
- Keep your presentation short and sweet. State your points succinctly and methodically, or your audience will give the telltale sign of impatience by looking at their watches.
- Use e-mails instead of calls and letters. They can cut down the response time threefold, and because everything is in writing, there is less chance of miscommunication.
- Keep your offering so short and pithy that it can be writ-ten on the back of a business card.

chapter 13

the desire to get the best that can be got

what marketers need to know

People who are driven to get the best that can be got spend more money on discretionary purchases—products that appeal to their emotions, desires, and passions. Getting the best that can be got is a matter of individual tastes and preference and it might not have anything to do with any practical consideration. Some would say that the Desire to Get the Best That Can Be Got Hot Button is based on a need for luxury. That may be, but it's only part of the equation. As people move up in life their tastes change. To the joy of hot button marketers, this hot button is also based on perceptions. It promises present and future emotional benefits that go way beyond the price.

how marketers can apply this

The drive to have the best that can be got is an insatiable hot button. Most often, savvy hot button marketers know that all they have to do is show consumers who are driven to have the very best a new and improved product (even a newer version of what they already have) and they will create a feeding frenzy. Of course, there's an element of comparison-shopping involved. And hot button marketers know that a solid side-by-side comparison is frequently all it takes to establish the positioning of the best that can be got product or service. This is also a situation where statistics and graphical analysis are great selling tools, especially among your technologically and scientifically inclined customers.

words that say it's the best that can be got	
new	latest
better than ever	most
finest	spectacular
greatest	ultimate
improved	ultra

the insatiable hunger for the very best

There is a certain mystique about buying the best one can reasonably afford. However, it's different from the desire for status. This hot button is not as much related to status as it is to self-achievement and knowledge. It's not about keeping up with the Joneses, because in our increasing isolation from our neighbors, we often don't know who the Joneses are, unless we meet them at some school function. According to the *New York Times*, people have become increasingly isolated from their neighbors in the last thirty years. Thus, people use television and magazines as reference points.

Also, with the availability and ease in procuring credit cards, many more people today can acquire the symbols and products of the wealthy, whereas they might not have been able to in the past. This new affluence has fostered a whole new level of desire across class groups. Coveting a neighbor's goods has been replaced by coveting the goods of the rich and the powerful as seen in the media. Meanwhile, the rich are looking elsewhere for their pleasures. In an article in the *New York*

Times, Dalton Conley, an author and a sociologist at New York University, said, "Whether or not someone has a flat-screen TV is going to tell you less than if you look at the services they use, and those who are serving them."

a desire for the "best that can be got" is internally driven

The "best that can be got" products and services are not built— they are defined by the purchasers. And they're something apart from simple conspicuous consumption. While conspicuous consumption is meant to show off wealth and power, buying the best that can be got involves owning a treasure strictly for the personal or physical satisfaction of owning the best.

In every category there is an "-est" factor. The products and services that satisfy this particular hot button are the brightest, fanciest, fastest in a given category—the quintessential. A quintessential product represents the perfect example of a class or quality. Buying the best that can be got is a tool of one-upmanship. You can't be one-upped if you have the finest. But more than that, owning the ultimate product or service gives a person a warm inner glow. It's also a way of showing affiliation, knowledge, and security—especially on the job. It's not what you put into a product. Like value, it's what your consumer takes out of it.

the quintessential product is the epitome of product satisfaction

The Harley-Davidson is the quintessential motorcycle even if, as a Harley engineer once said in *BusinessWeek*, "The new Japanese knockoffs are as good as, if not better than, Harleys." The vice president of sales for Kawasaki Motorcycles knows what he's up against: "The Harley audience buys on emotional and lifestyle issues." Harley-Davidson even tried to get a U.S. registration of what it refers to as its "trademark" distinctive engine rumble sound. It's the quintessential motorcycle sound—what all other motorcycle sounds are measured against.

The older people get, the more willing they are to splurge on things they denied themselves while the kids were at home. And buying the best is one of the things they splurge on. They waited years and years to buy a high-ticket item and now they want the best. A brand-new owner of a Harley—a woman of about sixty—explained her purchase simply and cogently: "I got me a Harley. Now I'm classy."

A quintessential product has an authenticity that transcends brands and frequently even its own trademarks. Often, when the brand tries to duplicate itself in other areas, the brand is not successful. Häagen-Dazs ice cream may be the quintessential dessert to some people, but when its marketers lent the Häagen-Dazs name to a new liqueur, sales didn't come close to expectations.

By the way, the anticipation of purchasing the quintessential product is often stronger than the actual product purchase. Also, the quintessential product in a category is not always the best, but the consumer is usually oblivious to—or ignores—the flaws because he or she is so emotionally vested. Here are some examples:

- Both Jaguars and Harleys have had a propensity for breaking down, but neither product has lost much of its cachet.

- To a pen fancier, the epitome of product perfection might be a Mont Blanc Diplomat, even though most owners complain that they leak, especially on airplanes.
- To a cooking fancier, it might be a Jenn-Air range, even though cheaper and better-performing ranges are available.
- To a knife fancier, it might be the Original Swiss Army Knife, even though many of the knockoffs are just as good.
- To someone who likes watches, it can be a Rolex. And yes, Timex watches are just as, if not more, accurate.

The point is this: The quintessential is not necessarily the best-performing product, but it has the perception in the minds of the buying market that it is the best. The one common denominator in quintessential products is that they give the buyer an emotional high—an emotional edge that can't be duplicated by any other brands. The products may not exceed expectations, but there is almost never any buyer's remorse.

how to spot the ultimate product

While the "best product that can be got" are true originals, they depend on certain factors. The first being consumer knowledge of the category. Consumers must know the category well so that they can opt for the best. If a consumer never uses a fountain pen, then he or she will never know the name Mont Blanc. A person who has never been on a motorcycle will never understand the appeal of a Harley.

The second factor is the symbolic power in the consumer's mind of the good or service. These products are far more than purveyors of utility. They serve both inner and outer expressive functions. What counts is how the product plays on the consumer's hopes, dreams, and self-image. Quintessential goods are a means of communication. They constitute a system of "signs" through which a purchaser makes statements about him or herself. While most status products are related to social status, these products signal allegiance to a particular lifestyle; and, they affirm that you are "in the know."

consumer self-identification and personality

Peter Burkhard of *www.burkhardworks.com* talks about different kinds of consumers and their mindsets. He mentions two different types of consumer profiles that want the "best you can get." Surprisingly, they are at opposite poles.

"The expressive consumer" responds to products and presentations that promise excitement and immediate emotional gratification. To sell to the expressive consumer, you try to evoke a smile. In fact, most "-est" products provoke a smile when the product is shown to them. For the expressive consumer, the product proclaims to people in similar peer groups that they have the knowledge to buy the best. Unlike products shown in the status sell, there is little ostentation. A middle-class consumer may want the new plasma TV because he gave in to an emotional rush when he saw it. He gets great pleasure seeing his wall covered in a new movie played on his new state-of-the-art DVD player. After all, it expresses his dreams and desires.

"The driver," on the other hand, is enthralled with competition. He or she is fast to act, quick to make a decision, cool, poker-faced, dispassionate. Drivers would rather be first than right. They fear losing out. They must have the quintessential because it shows that they are right—and successful. Once again, it's not about status, it's about fitting into the driver's personality.

A third type of consumer, not mentioned by Mr. Burkhard, is the inner-driven person. This person is self-involved, but not necessarily selfish. He or she tends to be introverted and doesn't care if anyone else sees the product. Self-satisfaction is most important to this person—he or she buys the product to fulfill a private dream and the reward is inner gratification. This person is prone to purchase "little treasures"—objects with a strong emotional pull, known only to the buyer.

the best that can be got on the job

On the job, getting "the best that can be got" can serve physical and psychological needs. If you're a professional and need a drill, you want to rely on the best because you're going to use it a lot. You need to spend money to make more money. You don't want to buy anything but the best, because if it lets you down when you're 500 feet up on a scaffold, it can mean big trouble.

Psychologically, if you are going to entrust your job to a product, it had better be the best. It impresses clients and coworkers. If you bid on a project or even show up for a meeting with anything but the best, it may put doubts in the client's mind. All things being equal, the person who drives up in the Mercedes will get the job over the one who drives up in a Chevy. Hirers want to buy from successful people. Showing up and *looking* successful usually means, to the buyer, that you *are* highly successful.

Yes, a quintessential product can actually close a sale. Always dress better than the client, even if it means dressing down. For instance, for formal business presentations, I dress in khaki pants and a sports shirt when I'm meeting people in formal three-piece suits. It's a bit of reverse psychology. If I position myself as the quintessential creative person, I have to look the part. When I made a successful presentation to Kellogg's, I was told that one of the reasons I got the project over the "suits" was because it showed I was successful and didn't need to impress them with the way I dressed. It showed my core competency. Business actually tripled when I stopped wearing custom suits.

Buying the best that can be got can help provide job security, too. It used to be said, that (in its halcyon days) nobody got fired for buying IBM. The company may have slipped since then, but when people in business buy "the best that can be got" and something goes wrong, they are held blameless. The corporate hirer can say he did his due diligence and brought in the right people and tools for the job.

Getting the best can also be a part of looking the part at work. When a pilot flies, there's a good chance he'll wear a special watch that other pilots wear, possibly a Rolex. He has to exude confidence and success to both his passengers and his peers. The Rolex shows his peers that he's part of the brotherhood of airline pilots. But his nonflying friends may have no clue that his watch is special, so he might wear a $10 watch when he's not working—that is probably more accurate anyway. He can wear the inexpensive watch because he's not trying to bond with a peer group.

getting the best that can be got isn't only about money

It may not be about money at all. Here's the key difference between getting the best that can be got and the prestige sell. The quintessential product makes the purchaser feel special about getting that something special. For instance, if one is a collector of books, or has even read a certain book, that person might enjoy a special edition with a gold leaf binding. It's the best edition that can be got. The book might be of no interest to anyone outside of that one individual. He or she may never show it to anyone else, but receives a psychic joy from owning it. The best that can be got is beyond money. It's beyond power. The quintessential product almost has a Dr. Feelgood quality about it.

nice-to-have vs. must-have

We talked in the first chapter about Must-Have versus Nice-to-Have. A quintessential pull is so strong that the consumer's *gotta have it*. The pull is so strong that some consumers can't even enter certain stores or Web sites because they get a Pavlovian response. They know before they go there that they're going to lose their sense of practicality because they want the product so much. They dare not enter the store for fear of spending too much money. Obviously Web site owners and shop owners like this. This kind of consumer can actually break into a sweat over a quintessential product that he or she's gotta have.

Everyone splurges on something that other people don't understand, and the product is more than a short-term reward. It's something that people take pride in owning. The more expensive, the better.

quintessential products have almost magical powers

Take the face cream industry. A tiny jar of Estée Lauder face cream costs about $75. Similar creams cost about half. The consumer says, "If it's so expensive, it must work." Consumers are quite willing to suspend certain beliefs when you develop the proper to-the-heart position and turn it into a quintessential product. I asked a consumer in a focus group for cosmetics about an antiaging product and why she was willing to spend $75 for it. She told me, "Suppose it *does* work. What if everyone buys it and uses it. Then their skin could look great (in a decade or so) and I'll look terrible." It was the best she could buy. "When I get older and see other people with younger faces, I'm going to wish I had bought it," she added.

Some would say that the Best That Can Be Got Hot Button is based on a need for luxury. That may be, but luxury is a moving target. Luxury is in the eyes of the beholder. As people move up in life their tastes change. At the same time advancements in technology, scientific discoveries, and product enhancements change. The best that can be got is constantly changing, but when you position your product as the "best that can be got," and continue to enhance it, all other products are no better than second-place finishers.

pushing the hot button

for marketers

- Create scarcity. Make sure your product is hard to get and hard to find. If everyone has it, it can't be that unique.
- Create a unique package with a unique appeal. Opening the package is part of the fulfillment of the buying experience.
- Never discount "Best You Can Get" products. This is different from discounting prestige. Part of the aura of a best you can get product is the price.

- Don't make many changes to best you can get products. Many people love their idiosyncrasies.

for salespeople
- Show how other people are all queuing up to buy the product and communicate the message "if you don't buy it now, you may not be able to find it in the future," or indicate that you may run out of it soon.
- Chances are you know about your product but you don't know how much emotion consumers invest in it. Spend time, especially for collectibles, showing the consumer the care that was put into manufacturing the product.
- Point out signatures and "certificates of authenticity."
- Find out why the consumer wants it so badly and build on what the consumer relates to you.

chapter 14

self-achievement

what marketers need to know

There was a headline in a recent issue of *Inc.* magazine that summed it up: "Picture Yourself a Success." It was the personification of the rewards of self-achievement. Self-achievement is a major goal for most people. There is a saying that goes, "It's not whether you win or lose, it's how you play the game." Not always so. To many people, winning is the most important part of a game, because it's a mark of self-achievement. The Self-Achievement Hot Button is a strong one.

how marketers can apply this

Create programs that encourage people to achieve their dreams—and then reward them for the progress they make. But first, get inside the head of your customer and find out exactly what his or her deepest desire is. Find out what would allow them to enjoy the kind of thrill that mountain climbers and world-class performers experience when they've done the impossible.

imagine this

Imagine you're climbing to the top of a mountain. Step by step, rock by rock, you're climbing your way to the top. You've eluded wind, rain, and being ravaged by the elements. You stand on the top. The view is electrifying, the air rarified. But even though the trip was glorious, that's not what made it stand out. It was the fact that you made it to the top.

Of course, not everyone can climb mountains. For some, climbing a small hill is just as thrilling. But, then, the hill doesn't have to be a physical hill. It can be a mental or emotional hill—such as the desire to get in shape, the desire to stand out from the mundane, or the desire to get praise from our bosses. Everyone has his or her own mountains to climb. In each case, getting to the top sparks the same sense of self-achievement that mountain climbers experience when they reach the top.

The Self-Achievement Hot Button, or the need for self-accomplishment, is universal. Its emphasis is on personal or psychological growth rather than material possessions or gains, although these are certainly among the trappings of success.

When we were kids, our teachers gave us gold stars and paper certificates when we did a task well. These made us feel that we had accomplished something. They were strong incentives that encouraged us to continue improving—especially when they won an exultant place on Mom's fridge. When we grew older and played sports, trophies for our sporting achievements took the place of gold stars. When we won a trophy, we held our heads a little higher. We walked a bit more confidently. Business psychologists know that as adults we seek praises from our bosses as much as we seek a good paycheck.

There's always a market for self-help books because people want to accomplish more and become better people. Accomplishments are symbols that exist in our psyches. A small project can be as rewarding as a life goal. Gaining success with a small goal allows people to experience the feeling of achievement.

Investing a small amount of time in a project seems more like entertainment. Time spent involved in the creation of something designed and made with one's own hands and ingenuity is extremely enjoyable. That's why craft shops like Hobby Lobby and Michael's are springing up seemingly everywhere.

self-achievement is wish fulfillment

Ask people what they want out of life. You will usually get an answer like "I want more success," "I want to get a promotion and make more money," or "I want a better relationship with my loved ones." If you ask them "Why?" they'll probably say something akin to "It feels good." Feeling good is the heart of success—it's the ultimate in self-achievement and success.

But what is success really? Although you may already have formed a picture in your mind of what success looks like, it still requires a simple definition. Ask ten people what success

---

real-life example   Mac Anderson started collecting quotations and motivational writings of the influential thinkers about twenty years ago. He believed that these writings, when gathered in one place, could help motivate and inspire others. In 1985, Mac and a small group of people designed and produced quote books and award plaques and customized gifts. Later, he created photographed, framed pictures. In 1988, he developed and mailed his first catalog. It was called "Celebrating Excellence." Yes, he used the Self-Achievement Hot Button to create a business and that success spawned more success. Today, his company, Successories, is the largest publisher of motivational media in the world. Successories' products are specifically designed to promote important organizational values of success throughout the workplace. According to the Successories Web site, they "motivate people to superior performance, and recognize individual and group achievements." What are these products really? Grown-up editions of the gold stars and certificates we got as kids. They still work. The people who receive them walk a little taller and more confidently.

means to them and chances are that you will get ten different answers. Then ask them, "What will success give you?" or "What will recognition give you?" They will usually arrive at one answer: "Feeling Good!" That's right. "Feeling Good" is the ultimate psychological need of any human being. However, despite our striving to feel good and to arrive safely and live in this ultimate mental and emotional comfort level, humans, almost paradoxically, have a yearning to improve themselves. If improving oneself means pushing beyond the boundaries of what's comfortable or what feels good, why do we do it?

In a word: self-achievement. Almost everyone would like to see some degree of improvement in the way we perceive ourselves. Now, we all know there is no wonder drug that will make us feel bold, smart, rich, and powerful; thus, we try to achieve self-esteem in big and small ways. We try to capture and show off the symbols of our success. However, we also need symbols to remind us *how* to succeed.

The following is not a generalization, although it sure sounds like one. *Everyone is trying to improve him or herself and accomplish something.* But, the answer to what makes a person feel special is in the head and heart of each individual consumer. The trick to finding the correct sales approach is to dig deep into your prospect's psyche. Perhaps your most important goal as a marketer or salesperson is to help your customers develop a sense of high self-esteem.

one way to do it is with an awards or rewards program

The strongest word in the human language is a person's name. The second strongest word is *you.* We love to hear the sound of our own name. That's why smart marketers greet their customers by name. This shows the consumer that he or she is valued and not just a money machine. Smart salespeople know that recognition is an important aspect of self-achievement and success.

How do you take advantage of this? Create an awards program for your clients. Sure, it may be a lot of work, but the benefit outweighs the effort invested. What can an award program do for you besides making your customers feel good? For starters it can lend instant credibility to you or your company. When I wrote for a magazine called *Food and Beverage Marketing*, we created an award called the Brammy for the brand managers of food and beverage companies. The Brammy made it easier to call on the award winners to buy ad space; and, because the award looked prestigious, both the magazine and the winner benefited from the borrowed prestige. The winners typically kept their Brammy Award in a place of importance; thus, the name of the magazine was always in front of them. Talk about great product placement!

success is in the minds of the achievers

You can think of all the hot buttons in this book as ways people try to further their accomplishments. No matter what a person does on the job, people seem to want to fulfill themselves by doing something else. This doesn't necessarily mean that they aren't fulfilled by their jobs. It simply affirms that the emotional electricity people get by accomplishing something is a unique kind of high.

Dave Barry, a syndicated humor writer, was called the "funniest man in America" by the esteemed television show *60 Minutes*.

Quite an accomplishment. But, according to his writings, he is more fulfilled when he's playing in a rock band. Bernie Williams, a star outfielder for the New York Yankees, gets a great rush of accomplishment when he plays his guitar for audiences.

The point is that "Be All That You Can Be" is more than a slogan for the Army. It's a way of life that people strive to achieve. The accomplishment can last as long as a minute or for an entire lifetime. The Self-Achievement Hot Button cuts through every known demographic.

the competition factor

The Self-Achievement Hot Button is at the heart of competitive situations. Many individuals respond to and take great delight in participating in competitive activities. It doesn't matter if it's the Olympics or a local arts and crafts competition. The challenges can, indeed, be compelling to those who enjoy pitting themselves against others. Even people who are not competitive in the traditional sense enjoy the thrill of victory in something they think they're good at, for instance—growing the biggest grapefruit at a local Grange Fair.

The best competitions—and this is particularly true of incentive programs—are those that create an environment that encourages and rewards multiple winners. Such programs give every participant the encouragement that they, too, can surely win something at some level. For example, in a golf tournament, awards might be offered for the lowest score, the best putt, longest drive, and closest to the hole. In sales incentive programs, the highest total sales production will certainly win the award, but others, such as the most improved production, and the greatest market share growth, could be recognized as well.

we all want to stand out in some aspect of our lives

Although we can't always get rave reviews from our bosses and reassuring hugs from our mates, we can feel special by buying and using a product based on self-achievement. Eateries have taken this to new heights as people segment themselves in castes in restaurants. Frequently you'll hear someone say, "Yes, I did something worthy of reward, so I can splurge on this pricey restaurant to go where the movers and shakers go." Or, "Yes, I deserve this platinum credit card, even though it costs more. I'm important and I'm worth it." In the travel industry getting down and dirty by sifting through dirt in an archaeological dig is an honor paid for by the same people who used to stay in Hiltons and out by the pool. Travel agencies are cashing in on the Self-Achievement and Discovery Hot Button at the same time.

and then there's self-expression

Self-expression is definitely another facet of the Self-Achievement Hot Button. Because self-achievement is wrapped up with a person's self-identity and their dreams of accomplishment, hot button marketers must pay special attention to a prospect's need for self-expression. Brand-equity guru David Aaker tells us that the way a brand or product feature expresses a customer's self-identify, or the way that customer wants to project him or herself to others, has a strong influence on the customer's response to the product. For example, a customer may try to look:

- Adventurous and daring by wearing a Rolex Mariner watch

- Successful and powerful by driving a Mercedes Benz
- Sophisticated by wearing Ralph Lauren clothes
- Caring and nurturing as a parent by serving Quaker Oatmeal
- Competent and risk-averse by purchasing IBM servers for the company

In this case the consumer chooses products for personal use because those products project to others a level of accomplishment that the individual has or aspires to achieve. The products serve as a reflection of what the consumer wants to express about herself to the outside world.

So, for an example, a runner who chooses to wear Saucony running shoes might choose them because they prefer the look and feel and its performance as a running shoe. But, an additional dynamic may also be at play here. Maybe a famous Olympic marathon runner also wears Saucony and the customer has chosen Saucony shoes to say, "I'm a dedicated, smart, serious runner, too."

another major hot button—breaking a bad habit

A subset of the Self-Achievement Hot Button is breaking a bad habit. A bad habit can be sloth, poor eating habits, smoking, or a myriad of other things the consumer finds disagreeable. In today's society bad habits are all considered character imperfections. Diet plans and smoking cessation programs are all being recycled as more people try to divest themselves of bad habits. The desire to break a bad habit and improve oneself in some way is a dream most of us aspire to achieve. When a consumer gets the results he wants—he gets a special satisfaction—and the Self-Achievement Hot Button is fulfilled.

A classic way to break a bad habit involves wearing a rubber band around your wrist as a constant reminder of the habit or craving that you're trying to beat. Unfortunately rubber bands are not high-ticket items. And, they break. People are most responsive to other people. So, they hire personal trainers and go to weight-loss clinics and antismoking groups. Peer pressure is important in helping people break bad habits. Probably the greatest example of this is Alcoholics Anonymous and some of the other twelve-step programs. The steps are important because getting past each one is a hill (a small success) that the person has to overcome to climb the mountain and achieve the ultimate success.

the marketer as enabler

I asked the president of a health club why people joined that club. I expected answers like "they want to be musclebound," "they're health nuts," or "to excel." But instead, he told me that most people want to tone up a bit and to be the best they can be. However, he explained that people have difficulty maintaining a program without support. While the machines were indeed available, it was more important that personnel were available to lend support and encouragement to the customers.

In a survey of the health club trade, people were asked, "What is the most important factor in keeping you happy at the club?" The answer given by 77 percent of the members was "the staffers." Why? Staffers cajoled, inspired, and empathized with the members. One person told me that when she missed a week at the gym, she'd get e-mail notices asking why. This made her feel good—somebody cared about her well-being. This one-to-one contact is also an important part of every major, legitimate diet program. They typically offer counselors or coaches that clients can identify with and turn to for guidance and encouragement. As a salesperson, you need to provide guidance and empower clients to achieve new heights. This can be as simple as calling after the sale to make sure everything is going well or as complicated as doing additional research in your client's area to further the buyer's growth.

tips and tricks to help your prospects achieve new heights

Here are some real-life observations from focus groups we've held for self-improvement products and services. They'll give you some helpful insights into how to market to the Self-Achievement Hot Button consumer, regardless of what your product and/or service might be.

become a personal trainer/coach

In fact, those words should always be used together. While consumers prefer to talk to their trainer/coach in person, the phone and the Internet should also be used to maintain contact. Although consumers don't expect to get the same person every time (although they would ideally like to), they would like a person with access to their records. Once again, there are technologies that allow this over the Internet.

make your web site user-friendly and likeable

They should show real people and real trainers. They might even include films showing how to do particular exercises. In focus groups, a concept board showing a woman looking at an actual person over the Internet scored well.

personalize all advertising and promotions

Don't just show products and the plan. Show everyday people in happy real-life situations. The people used should be reasonably fit but not overly musclebound. If they're too "perfect" consumers won't relate. The people who want to be "hunks" are not going to be a major part of your member mix anyway.

Despite the fact that most people we interviewed had recently bought some kind of fitness machine or apparatus, most of the time it gathers dust. Almost every person in almost every group said they felt the need for some kind of motivation to use the equipment. Furthermore, most felt only a real person could provide this motivation.

To summarize, personal growth is important to everyone. Show how your product can add to a person's goals and self-image. Even a mundane product like deodorant can take on new meaning when you show how the deodorant will keep an executive "cool" during business meetings. Become a hero by inspiring your clients to "climb that mountain."

pushing the hot button

for marketers

- Show how the consumer earned the product and the praise—usually as a self-reward for doing something.
- Give the consumers tools to customize a particular product.

- Create "kit" products to build on the self-esteem of putting something together.
- Hold contests for the best and most creative ways to use the product. Display the results on a Web site.

for salespeople
- Create rewards for different levels of skill in incentive programs. It keeps the programs interesting and ensures the same person doesn't win every time.
- Set benchmarks for all your self-esteem products, preferably written out, so achievers can see their progress.
- Don't forget those certificates and gold stars.

chapter 15

sex, love, and romance

what marketers need to know

The use of sexual imagery in marketing will ebb and flow, but it will never disappear completely. The simple truth is that sex sells. Eric Zanot, an instructor in advertising at the University of Maryland, has said: "There is always going to be sex in advertising for the simple reason that it's just one of our basic strong emotions." Advertisers are always looking to attach their products to basic emotions because emotions are what sell products. Sex engages the consumer's deepest emotions immediately and in a primal sense—in a way that no other hot button can.

Love, as well as sex, is certainly a strong emotional driver and we'll address it in a bit. But an ad focused on the primal instincts works faster—especially for men. The fact is that you, as a hot button marketer, can create a strong positioning for your product by building on lust.

how marketers can apply this

The desire to love and be loved is a strong hot button. In addition to outward and obvious displays of sex, show how your product will make a person be loved a bit more or show how love can be given and you'll win the heart of the consumer. Sex and love can be used in a number of ways to sell products. It all depends on the product, and the gender. For ads aimed at men, romance is usually not a primary approach. Instead, the approach is sex without any complications or difficulties. For women it's hearts, flowers, and romance. But women are now also responding to more obvious sexual imagery. Be it for men or women, sex will always sell.

primal instincts

Birds do it. Bees do it. According to the *New York Times*, even blue-green algae do it.

Do what? Bond with each other—in order to have baby algae. According to an article in the *Times*, blue-green algae have to get together in order to reproduce. Of course, scientists know that blue-green algae are asexual beings and reproduce by cloning themselves. But what they now understand is that when these algae want to reproduce they gather together as a group—even though there is no sexual reproduction involved! They still need or want the energy of others to reproduce. Something like a one-celled singles bar.

Sexual interest and romantic interest are two of the most basic emotions. After all, without reproductive urges there would be no human race. (Which would mean no customers and then you wouldn't be able to sell anything.) Selling through sex is a way of getting consumers to involve their emotions, minds, and yearnings in a product or ad. This is a triad of emotions that is rather hard to beat.

what has *cosmo* wrought?

Cosmopolitan magazine helped break many cultural taboos when it changed the focus of its material to be almost exclusively about sex. The magazine that appealed to women featured stories about sex that were even more blatant than the ones found in *Playboy*. Female consumers, as a whole, have evolved in their openness to sexual discussion and their responses to sexual appeals in marketing in the past few decades. Just look at the magazines that appeal to women at the supermarket checkout stand today. Here are some current headlines.

"We'll Take Your Love Life to a Whole New Level"

"27 Things You Need to Know to Have Great Sex"

"99 Ways to Touch Him"

"Big Sex News"

"Cheap Little Seduction Tricks"

While studies have shown that men are most responsive to sexual images and stimuli, women do, indeed, respond to blatant sexual appeals and images. Calvin Klein set the tone with sexy male models clad in briefs. At the time it was a groundbreaking strategy because the ads were the first to use an almost naked man to get attention. And to think that the women's magazines once attracted attention by offering the best chocolate cake recipes!

sex, the vcr, and the internet

Pornographic tapes initially appealed mainly to the prurient interest in men. In fact, pornographic tapes were in large part responsible for the explosive growth of videotape recorders during their introductory phase. For the first time, men didn't have to show their faces in fourth-rate theaters in seedy neighborhoods. They could actually buy sexual material at the local deli or video store. But porn purveyors found that men and women wanted different types of material. Men wanted traditional sex scenes and explicit material. Women wanted sex scenes that placed more emphasis on romance. Men and women had the same hot button—but different drivers.

A major driver of the development of the Internet's technology came from the sex sites. Adult entertainment sites were, and still are, ahead of the curve in terms of marketing to their consumer base. They've capitalized on technical and marketing methods, including video streaming, faster downloading techniques, and live Internet conversations. Adult sites were the first to market videoconferencing over ordinary phone lines. The upshot is that traditional marketers have adapted such methods to sell their (non-sex-related) products.

using sex to sell is hardly new

While sexual images are rampant in today's marketing and advertising, many people incorrectly consider it a recent event and proof that society is going to hell in a handbag. The images may be more blatant now, but pictures of sex acts were being drawn on cave walls back when implements to do so were first invented. Michelangelo, Botticelli, and other great artistic masters used nudity in their paintings and statues during the Renaissance, as did the Romans and Greeks long before

marketing insight   In nearly all the marketing interviews I've conducted with women on the subject of sex, physical appearance plays a major part in the attraction. In the real world, dungarees or Levis were not exactly "slim cut" or sexy; they were stiff and probably dirty. Few real cowboys fit the image of the Marlboro Man, but our fantasy cowboy has a lean backside in a pair of tight-fitting jeans, long legs, and that ever-present Stetson. A pair of chaps invariably draws the eyes to the uncovered sections of denim. Physical appearances and what used to be called "lewdness" now attract modern women as well as they always have for men.

them, for commercial as well as aesthetic applications. Posters showing buxom, and almost topless, women were used to sell tobacco products in the nineteenth century. A Midwestern varnish company used completely nude models in the 1930s.

What the savvy hot button marketer needs to understand is that hitting the customer's hot button isn't just about explicit sexual images in products and advertising. *It's about making a person more attractive and more appealing to the opposite sex.* Consumers want to feel they are desirable. If your product can offer even the illusion of that, you'll have something pretty powerful.

Sex and romance works—and science has actually proven it. When a person is shown an image of sex or erotica, brain scans reveal that particular regions of the brain light up; but when the same person is shown images of love and romance, a totally different section is highlighted on the scan. This phenomenon happens with both males and females. Thus, when you show sex and love in your marketing program or ad, you're essentially stimulating two sections of your customer's brain!

promises of love and sex are stimulating and motivating

Marketing campaigns use promises of romance and love to sell just about everything. This may be a more subtle means of persuasion than using images of nudity, but the underlying themes are much the same. Selling through sex and romance is also an aspirational sell. The women and men in most of the ads are idealized in face and physique. *Playboy* magazine revealed the effectiveness of the airbrush in ridding their models of imperfections. Advertising agencies use casting companies and makeup artists to do the same. In addition, the men in such advertisements are usually depicted as impeccably coiffed and, apparently, rich—just the right material for breeding a proper family, according to Robert D. Leonard and Marcel Harmon of the University of New Mexico's Department of Anthropology. Again, the ads look to hit on primal instincts. Once again, it is the dream being sold, not the reality. (Obviously when we buy a car we're not guaranteed to also get the bikini-clad model who is leaning against the car.) In commercials, nobody fights or argues and the object of the sexual fantasies always behaves like we want them to behave. If only real life were that easy.

sex as status

It is relatively easy to sell many products via a sexual connection; however, such a connection is usually easier to set up for male consumers given their stronger responses to visual images. At the time this is being written, Paris Hilton is being shown in a commercial washing a car to sell hamburgers. Even the basic premise that the ultra-rich Hilton would be washing her own car is ludicrous. But the appeal is easy. According to author Richard F. Taflinger, men don't have a great deal of criteria for sexual desire. Show a young woman with a good anatomy and

---

marketing insight   Is there too much sex in advertising? *Adweek* magazine ran a poll asking consumers if there was too much sex in advertising, and 73 percent of responders said no. Furthermore, they asserted that sexy ads don't actually affect them. They're lying. Or they just don't understand. Brain scans indicate enhanced activity in certain regions of the brain when consumers are shown sexy ads. Sex is one of our primary impulses, even if we don't know what is happening.

she is desirable. Hilton is playing on man's natural impulses rather than his thought processes, which would undoubtedly see the ludicrousness of the premise. The Hilton ad doesn't discuss her qualification for knowing hamburgers, nor her expertise in washing cars. Despite the viewers' fantasies, we don't even know that she would be a good lover. But that's not the point. Just her being there is enough to capture the attention of the male consumer.

So, why did this advertiser spend a great deal of money to feature a nearly naked Hilton washing a car with only a logo of the fast-food chain on the screen and a hamburger? Because consumers respond to sexual stimuli. If the company were to put a commercial on TV of a man sitting alone at a fast-food counter, devouring a hamburger, not many men would find that appealing. But Hilton (or any attractive woman) demands attention. Suddenly a hamburger is not just about satisfying hunger—it's a vehicle to satisfy desire. The advertiser is playing to the consumer's sexual and emotional, rather than physical, hunger.

the best ads suggest the possibility

In recent years, the trend in advertising and marketing has been to show a man and a woman together, in sexually charged circumstances. Despite women's increased acceptance of more blatant sexual images, female consumers are more responsive to ads that suggest the *possibility* of something. If you use this approach, you can sell almost anything. While I have never seen a sexual approach sell pancake batter, it could be done if you show a scene of an attractive man and woman dressed in pajamas, with the man cooking pancakes for the woman. A strong and selling ad allows viewers to use their imaginations about what might have happened before—or what might happen after. So the commercial might work on two levels: one, the implied romanticism; and two, the image of the pancake batter is changed from an ordinary breakfast product to one that can have romantic connotations.

sex is marketing to the heart for women

Although women do have instinctive sexual reactions, the emotional support given by a partner is usually more compelling to them. Money, power, and prestige—i.e., the hot buttons in this book—are factors that women define as extremely valuable. However, because these are not always conscious desires, they must be intimated rather than actually shown. For example, in order to sell diamonds, marketers use a romantic approach. The majority of diamonds are sold to men; however, men buy them for the women in their life, not for themselves. The woman usually makes the purchase decision, although it's the male consumers actually spending the money. Thus, the images in diamond commercials and in magazines appeal to women. The lighting is soft, the ambience is saturated with elegance, the man is obviously nurturing and well-to-do. Even in sex and romance, hot button marketers must market to aspirational qualities. In the pancake example, the man is shown as responding to the woman's wants and needs. We may not see sex in the ads, but the signs are there, subtle and disguised.

love is in the air . . . for men and women

Everyone wants to be loved. Everyone wants to be desired. Everyone wants romance, even though men and women define it differently.

Consider the following ad scenarios:

- A woman and man lie in bed discussing insurance and their future.
- A Coors Light ad advises women to keep their figures to attract men.
- Perfume ads and lotion and potion marketing imply that the products are magic elixirs that attract the opposite sex. In fact, most perfume ads sell romance rather than perfume.

These all show how a woman can attract a man—and vice versa. The difference is the way the ads attract men and women. Ads aimed at men usually show sex to attract attention. Successful ads aimed at women will show the possibility of bedding down. It may happen, it may not, but sex is not the main point. Thus, sex can be explicit or implied. According to Richard F. Taflinger, men want more explicit images, and women want more subtle images.

Sex will sell because it plays on a man and a woman's natural instincts. There will always be people who oppose sex in advertising because they consider it demeaning to men and women. But how sex is accepted in advertising, and in the media in general, has been changing rapidly. Women are more open to sexual messages. Men have always been open. Love and sex have been strong motivating forces since the beginning of time. We can't ignore them, because they have a pull like no other marketing tool. When properly researched and executed, it is a hot button that marketers can use to generate greater sales.

pushing the hot button

for marketers
- Sell differently to men and women. Although the goals may be similar, they take pleasure in different things, so market to that.
- Fantasy is a powerful marketing tool. As Victoria's Secret has shown, hiding small areas of flesh can be more arousing than showing everything.
- Create products and marketing that provide hope that one will succeed in getting the partner they want.

for salespeople
- Create tension by alluding to the idea that the opposite sex is being won away by another person.
- In retail stores, show men what their woman wants. Men are usually clueless about these purchases.
- Don't be afraid to ask questions about body types, intimate habits, a partner's personality type, etc. Sex has come out of the closet. Don't assume your prospect will be afraid to talk about it.
- Assume the attitudes of the person you are trying to persuade. It will give you a better handle on what to sell.

chapter 16

the nurturing response

what marketers need to know

When pushed correctly, the Nurturing Hot Button is a strong one that can be applied to a vast array of products and sales pitches. As a marketer or salesperson, you might need to do some thinking on how to appeal to this hot button effectively, because the nurturing aspects of your product may not always be readily apparent. You'll want to remember that while the Nurturing Hot Button appeals slightly more to women (perhaps due to their roles as caregivers), men can respond to this hot button, too. Nurturing can also be strong when we play on a person's guilt and imply a worst-case scenario for a loved one. A human's need to care for others' well-being can be just as important as the urge to receive care.

how marketers can apply this

Nurturing is about doing something for someone else. Many products can be used with the nurturing sell. Play up what your product or service can help the customer do for others. As with the Family Values Hot Button, don't be afraid to get sappy. People respond to it. You can also tap into the Nurturing Hot Button by selling a product under the guise of learning—mothers, in particular, will respond to the pitch. In selling via the

Nurturing Hot Button, the trick is to make Mom and Dad the hero, not the product.

how it works

It was some time ago when I learned how important the Nurturing Hot Button is, even in the most common of product categories. I was speaking to a young woman when I developed a new kid's toothpaste for Colgate-Palmolive. Initially, we weren't even trying to develop a toothpaste specifically marketed to kids. We were trying to develop any kind of toothpaste that could make money for Colgate and that their salespeople could sell without a great deal of resistance from retailers or buyers. Colgate was tired of losing profits and market share to Crest.

The young woman was a receptionist in our office. We had literally hundreds of ideas and concepts pinned to the wall, focusing on taste, therapeutic appeal, or anything we could add to the product to potentially make it more sellable. She looked at them and said they were cute, but meaningless and insignificant, at least to her. Being curious about her response, I asked why.

The woman said many of her friends were unwed mothers or first-time mothers. They wanted assurance and reassurance that they were providing the best of care for their children. They wanted a toothpaste that spoke to their needs, and to their children's needs, in a noncondescending way. We had been so preoccupied considering what the taste and texture of the product should be that we had missed an unmet psychological need just waiting to be fulfilled. There was a whole segment of consumers who wanted to feel good knowing they were doing their job well. We extended the concept and found that most mothers had the same concern. Out of this project

Colgate Jr. (originally named First Brush) and a whole line of oral care products positioned to moms—for their children—was developed.

In *Parents* magazine as well as other publications, Procter & Gamble promotes the benefits of young fathers (rather than a mother in a prim housedress) holding the baby. More and more marketers of children's goods are appealing jointly to mothers and fathers. To be politically correct is to embrace one's sensitive side—to be nurturing.

The Nurturing Hot Button is about the need to give care, comfort, growth, and support to others. Nurturing is about the need to see living things thrive and progress—to provide security, to protect one's charges from harm and injury. Nurturing is an innate, instinctive emotional response in most of us. You can learn the hows and whys of nurturing, but you're usually born with the desire. Many animal species are born with a similar instinct; however, it is not as well defined or long lasting as in humans.

Scientists believe that even robot pets trigger a hard-wired nurturing response in humans. MIT anthropologist Sherry Turkle, one of the leading researchers in the field, is conducting studies on how children perceive smart toys like AIBO, FURBY, Tamagotchi, and My Real Baby. She asserts that humans are programmed to respond in a caring way to creatures, even brand-new artificial ones. Nurturing is about both physical and emotional growth. Who doesn't smile when the commercial for a child's disposable underpants comes on and the child proudly says, "I did it myself"? It's easy to relate to.

The nurturing response is one of the great pulls in life. Band-Aids, Lucky Dog dog food, and even Miracle-Gro plant food are sold on the basis of nurturing. Whole industries have sprung up by pushing the Nurturing Hot Button. A big growth sector exists for high-priced dog foods that consumers perceive as better for their pets than mass-produced dog foods with funny names. The ads always point out the caring relationship owners have with their pets.

myself as hero

Relationships are a key component of the Nurturing Hot Button. When Mom and Dad see themselves as heroes for choosing the product, this pushes the hot button. In terms of communications and selling, hot button marketers should not use the classic product-as-hero strategy. Seeing the product as the hero—the way most consumer products are promoted— can actually be a big mistake. The customer is the nurturer or healer for CHOOSING the product—not your product itself.

Call it the Doctor Syndrome. When one goes to the doctor and gets a penicillin shot, is the penicillin treated as the hero? No. It is the doctor who is considered heroic for having the knowledge to prescribe the drug. A successful nurturing approach idealizes the consumer as nurturer or caregiver. When one goes to a nurturing institute like a preschool, we talk about the teachers, not the books they use. The Colgate product worked because moms found the product that appealed to their needs. It was Mom who found a way to get her children to brush their teeth willingly.

some nurturing categories and sells are obvious—some are not

The obvious products associated with nurturing include those for birthing, child care, pet care, cooking, and even laundry.

Yes, washing clothes, mundane a necessity as it is, carries a ton of emotional hot buttons and nurturing cues. That's why laundry makers add scents to their products. To stretch the market further, plants and garden items, charities, and "feel-good" companies can be included. Goodwill Industries is a great example of operating as a "feel-good" company. It operates on the premise of helping (nurturing) poor people. In reality, they are a for-profit business that sells used goods. But they use the nurturing appeal so well, people don't even question that Goodwill Industry's sole purpose is to nurture the less fortunate.

administering care vs. getting cared for

The desire to give care is strong. Perhaps it's as strong as—or stronger than—the urge to receive care. Who has not looked at a critically ill loved one and wished that it were he or she lying in the hospital bed instead? Empathy and empathetic situations are key drivers of the nurturing response. If we feel empathy toward a person who needs help, we are more likely to help them. Our desire to nurture is almost always in proportion to the empathy felt.

Even the insurance business has replaced the classic approach of negative selling for the empathetic approach. There are no

---

marketing insight   Want a quick trick you can use to make your ads and promotional material evoke empathy and the nurturing response? Put people with big eyes in your ads—especially children. Even in dog food ads, show a dog with large eyes. According to Michael C. LaBarbera, in an article in *Psychology Today*, there's something about big eyes that brings out the nurturing person within us. That's why E.T. had big eyes . . . and all the bad guys in Steven Spielberg movies have little beady ones.

more pictures or imagery of poor old dad going to the Great Spirit in the Sky. Insurance companies, for the most part, have eliminated the former negative hot button of "what happens if you die" and "slice of death" approaches. They have replaced them with the Nurturing Hot Button. Their messages now tell us that we can provide for our children and loved ones under any conditions. Buying their product becomes a way consumers can nurture their loved ones.

AOL Time Warner and CIGNA harnessed the Nurturing Hot Button by pooling their resources. They created consumer awareness and a strong brand affinity when they created a message to show they were in the "Business of Caring." CIGNA developed a program called the "The Power of Caring," which sponsored advertorials in different AOL Time Warner media. The campaign featured personalities involved with good causes. By identifying lifestyle junctures such as parenting, retirement, home planning, and money management, AOL Time Warner targeted those predisposed to CIGNA's messages. The program achieved outstanding results, not only exceeding brand awareness goals, but also in delivering high levels of reader recall. Charities taking part in the campaigns also saw an increase in donations as a direct result of the campaign—which was hot button marketing at its best.

The trend toward functional foods is also driven by the nurturing instinct. Marketers convey health benefits by adding or concentrating ingredients in foods and beverages that can prevent or treat illness and disease and/or promote health and well-being. Now someone paying their neighbor a friendly visit stands as much chance of getting a multivitamin drink as a cup of coffee. For years the functional food market in the United

States tended to be associated with lifestyle and convenience, but psychologists have learned a stronger driving motivation could be found by giving the family something to eat that might prevent disease. Its satisfaction derived from providing wholesome food for others.

the laying on of hands

Nurturing is a touchy-feely kind of emotional hot button. Physical touch is a primary way that humans express caring. This same kind of sell can be extended to beauty parlors, spas, and massage therapies. *Beauty* magazine says that in order for a salon to be successful, the atmosphere needs to be calming, soft, and nurturing. The laying on of hands nurtures the soul as much as it nurtures the body. We feel good from the inside out and from the outside in.

Vicks uses the sensation of personal touch to great results. The television commercials for Vicks VapoRub depict kids and cold sufferers looking miserable and barely able to rouse their head from the pillow. VapoRub evokes an immediate need to help the victim and it always involves rubbing the product on the body of the child or a loved one. Who hasn't had a cold? Who hasn't been miserable?

The Nurturing Hot Button in this commercial works on four levels:

- It involves the laying on of hands, and the enjoyment and comfort of the same.
- It shows the characters in an empathetic situation.
- It involves making someone feel better—the essence of nurturing.

- It reminds target viewers of the moments when they were being nurtured by their parents with Vicks.

The same basic approach can be used with the nurturing effects of tea (which Mom probably made you drink when you had a cold), soups (a nourishing and nurturing experience), and even a baseball game. Many people remember their parents nurturing them by taking them on a family outing or to a game. They may not *consciously* link the act to nurturing, but the pull is strong nonetheless.

how to use the nurturing hot button in communications

According to *Circulation Management* magazine, the nurturing appeal seemed a natural for promoting a book from Rodale (the publishers of *Prevention* magazine) called *The Doctors Book of Home Remedies for Dogs and Cats*. However, the lack of emotion in the posed pictures of women and their dogs resulted in less-than-stellar results.

When it came time to promote a new magazine, *Pets: Part of the Family*, a candid photo of a woman kissing her sled dog was used to complement the headline "Pure Love," and the response was much more positive.

Choosing the right environment and colors for nurturing communications can provide visual clues and help your message to be heard. According to one study, pink indicates a strong personality. It suggests femininity, gentleness, well-being, and innocence. Pink is considered emotional in character and connotes a sensitive heart. The affectionate and concerned individual prefers pink. Gently, you offer love, attention, and nurturing to those in distress and needing guidance. For business, however, you must be aware of the color's feminine links and implications.

Showing people at play is also a way to promote the nurturing hot button. Play is seen as a way to re-establish a connection after a relationship has taken a wrong turn. We can get things back on track with children by playing with them. It can be much more effective than yelling at them or lecturing them, or telling them how frustrated we are. Likewise, playing with a customer's kids in a selling situation can create a bonding nature and can help you close a sale.

nurturing applies to a wide variety of demographics and products

Who does not feel guilty when they pass over the numerous ads for charities to feed hungry children? How you tie into the nurturing aspect of your product depends on the age and sex of your target group. For instance, single women in their thirties are often ruled by their biological clocks. Many products for this market segment should be tied into the joy of having and nurturing children.

Products to be considered under the needs for nurturing include:

- Those that give care—products like Theraflu
- Those that can provide comfort—comfort foods like potatoes and pasta
- Those that provide growth to all living things (Think of a set of encyclopedias and how you felt you were enriching your children's lives by buying it.)

Lever Brothers created the name Snuggle for their fabric softener and gave it a nurturing appeal. The teddy bear symbol/spokes-animal they developed played right into our ever-lovin', nurturing hearts.

successful nurturing approaches

The baby boomers—still a growth market—are a new target for products of a nurturing nature, because many of them are grandparents or will be soon. They are prime targets for a "grandma purchase." These are products that are too expensive—or even too esoteric—for the parents to buy themselves. These can be expensive toys, books, and even video games. Toy makers have learned to tie the sell into a learning experience, which is part of the Nurturing Hot Button. Nourishing young minds is the ultimate nurturing act.

Travel can also be viewed as a nurturing experience. Club Med started out as a swinging singles haven. These singles eventually married and had children. (As an effect of Club Med, perhaps?) Club Med now positions some of its clubs as places for families to come together. They feature crafts, movies, and the opportunity to learn a foreign language—thus, travel becomes a learning experience for the entire family.

PPP, a product and marketing company run by Judi Cohen, markets many products under the nurturing banner. She has developed little stickers as toilet-training aids. The child gets the sticker when he uses the toilet correctly. One of the ways she marketed the product was to give out coupons for the product to manufacturers. Sales proved excellent. She has since expanded into behavior modification products that allow parents to gently correct a child's inappropriate behavior and is working with Wal*Mart to develop a parenting section in stores.

Even a product as mundane as shoelaces can be marketed as a nurturing experience. Ms. Cohen also markets elastic shoelaces that she bills as being so easy, children don't get frustrated tying their shoes. Shoes, themselves, can be a nurturing target. Stride Rite has built their whole company by assuring moms that Stride Rite promotes proper foot growth.

the nurturing approach carries through categories and product lines

You might say, "I own a business that has nothing to do with nurturing"—a technology business, for example. Well, consider this: A large part of the growth of Apple computers was attained by using the nurturing hot button. Apple computers made special deals with schools to provide them with low-cost computers. AOL offers special grants to the needy to supply computers and special sections for kids.

On a much smaller scale, one tiny computer service company, The Friendly PC, offers to help nurture beginners slowly, getting people past their anxiety over computers. This company

marketing insight   Many people go into the teaching profession because they want to nurture young minds. Teachers are always a strong sales prospect for the Nurturing Hot Button sell. Businesspeople want to nurture others by means of mentoring programs. The president of a local chamber of commerce put it this way, "We ran a business seminar and had about fifty requests to teach something." People in business often want to mentor or teach others about their business. In fact, most cities have institutions called Incubators to nurture small businesses and their entrepreneurs.

tries to get the kids into the computer lessons at the same time as their moms and dads, making the business of learning a bonding experience for the family. The company has also compiled a list of Web sites that offer safe games, educational material, and other entertainment strictly for kids.

You can take advantage of the nurturing hot button by donating a portion of your sales to a needy-kids' home, an animal shelter, or any other company that helps people.

girl scout cookies—merchandising angle or a true nurturing experience?

Girl Scout Cookies are the epitome of hot button marketing. The entire concept of the product is built on the nurturing response. When you buy a box of cookies, you think you're contributing to the emotional growth of a young girl. It's "myself as hero" again. The Girl Scout Cookie drive is a marketing phenomenon. Supermarkets will let the Girl Scouts stand in front of their stores and sell, even if it negatively impacts the store's own cookie sales! The customers that buy the Girl Scout Cookies, and the store's PR department, feel that they are enriching the kids' hearts and minds. The fact that they are doing a good deed also doesn't go unnoticed by the community and their customer base. Can you imagine a cookie company like Nabisco getting the same rights and privileges? Most fundraising programs aimed at school children espouse the benefits of the kids learning and growing from the selling experience as much as they play up the money raised for equipment and activities. That's probably true, but, ironically enough, they're often selling candy or other nutrient deficient products that

Mom would never let into the house—unless it's under the Nurturing Hot Button, that is.

guilt as a hot button

You can also evoke the Nurturing Hot Button by implying a worst-case scenario. What happens if the consumer does not buy a certain product or service? Will they, or a loved one, be adversely affected? This works best if you imply the negative, rather than say it. If you play on the negative hot button too hard, you run the risk of consumers resenting you and your product. There is evidence, for example, to suggest that positive messages about nurturing are generally more effective than messages that blame or frighten.

Michelin has been playing on the consumer's guilt for years. Michelin Tires gets more mileage from its "baby sitting in a tire" commercials than larger tire manufacturers whose products offer many more details and specifications. Look at the implied meaning. God forbid you get into an accident—with your child in the car—because you didn't buy Michelins.

It has been proven time and time again that children learn at their own pace. Buying toys that foster creativity will not make your child smarter in the long run. Buying a toy that can help your child spell "cat" or count to eleven as a toddler may make for a neat parlor trick, but the intelligence factor is pretty much going to even out as the child gets older. But here's the rub. What if little Johnny down the street has the Little Scientist Creation Lab and your kid doesn't? Is little Johnny going to be the first on the block to cure cancer while yours plays with pickup sticks? Heaven forbid. What if you don't send your child to the very best preschool? What if he doesn't read *War and Peace* in kindergarten? Almost all parents think their child is gifted. To buy a toy that has nothing but play value is seen as a negative—and not nurturing at all. These products sell as much on negative nurturing as well as positive nurturing. It's a good thing if you can put both emotions into your sell.

guilt nurturing: part two—safety guilt

Shelley Hunter, mother of three, and an author of a forthcoming book called *Businesses for Working Moms*, writes about something called "safety guilt." She talks about a time when outlets were uncovered and cabinets were unlocked. People are a great deal more safety conscious today—all under the auspices of the Nurturing Hot Button. There are outlet covers, crib tents, stair gates, bumper pads, bath rings, and at least a hundred other safety items. Are these items totally necessary or just the result of product companies capitalizing on the guilt aspect? No one can say for sure, but what marketers know for sure is that people picture the "what-if" scenario. If anything were to happen to their child and they had bypassed the product that would have saved him or her, the mother would forever flash back to that moment in Babies 'Я' Us when she decided that $5.99 was too much to pay for the child's safety. So, consumers, once again, buy the product as an insurance policy—"safety guilt."

Nurturing is an important value in all cultures. Turn on the TV and watch a boy playing with a dog. Walk through Babies 'Я' Us and you'll find toys to stimulate and enchant, videos to soothe and calm, games that teach. Tour the grocery aisle and you'll find satisfying comfort foods. Nurturing is an inner driver that allows both the nurturer and the nurturee to grow and to negotiate the world just a little bit better. Nurturing makes an overwhelming appeal to the heart.

pushing the hot button

for marketers

- Give your product a new look that resembles something alive. It appears some robot vacuum cleaner owners are becoming emotionally attached to their machines, almost as if they were alive. Scientists have already noticed that robot pets tap into a hardwired human nurturing response. It now looks like robot vacuums are unintentionally doing the same. One source says that the look of Macintosh Computers evokes the nurturing response.
- Use problem/solve solutions in communications. Show one family member tending for another. Kodak is running a commercial of a little kid looking for his dog. It's simple, emotional, and effective.
- Use emotions and simplicity. Employ bare-bottomed babies, singing kids, big-eyed dogs, and fluffy animals. They may be used often, but they still connote nurturing. Hospitals now use the Nurturing Hot Button on younger and older patients by suggesting patients bring their favorite blankets and pillows. Some open-heart surgical hospitals now actually provide Care Bears for their patients to soften the sterile hospital environment with a warm and nurturing feeling.
- Target revaluers (baby boomers) for nurturing products like expensive toys. They have the money and emotional commitment for these purchases.

- Sponsor nurturing organizations and have the good feelings transferred to you. These organizations might include tutoring programs and animal sanctuaries. Better yet, partner with them.

for salespeople
- Sell toys that feature a learning experience.
- Talk about how your product or service can enhance a child's or family's health and well-being.
- Volunteer for mentoring groups and youth groups. This can immediately give your prospects a warm feeling about you.

chapter 17

reinventing oneself

what marketers need to know

People reinvent themselves for many different reasons. For some, it's the sudden realization that they're not happy or fulfilled. Others reinvent themselves as a natural step in their growth. Reinvention can happen at almost any age; it's been said that we all go through seven-year life cycles. Reinvention is most apparent in adolescents and young adults moving out of childhood who are seeking to identify and define who they are and want to be. However, reinvention occurs at any age and is a basis for the revaluing demographic addressed earlier in the book.

how marketers can apply this

Most often people don't change unless they are uncomfortable. If everything is going smoothly, there is no impetus to change. It's a fact of life that, for most people, things don't go well all of the time. People lose jobs, fall in and out of love, experience financial setbacks, and get older. The discomfort of life's events drives people to change and reinvent themselves. Typically, people are more motivated by the desire to avoid pain than to gain pleasure. They strive to forget past hurts and discomfort. Your job as a hot button marketer is to salve the wounds and help to ease the transition. But first, you need to understand the commitment level of the individual. Are they really serious about reinventing themselves? If so, then your job as a hot button marketer or salesperson is to help them.

words that speak of reinventing oneself	
begin	new
beginning	now
create	pretend
imagine	start
introducing	today
launch	you can
never before	why not?

wishful thinking

Wouldn't it be great if life came with a chalkboard and an eraser? We could wipe away our mistakes and nobody would ever know that we made any. Over time we would forget them, too. How many people wish they could start out with the wisdom they've built up over the years without going through all the turmoil it took to acquire it? Successful hot button marketers offer products and services that help people "start over" and find new ways to improve their lives. Marketers speed this process along by finding a way, or creating products or services, that can help someone create a "new you."

Consumers and business buyers carry a great deal of physical and emotional baggage with them. A trip or vacation can help a person start over or at the very least it can symbolize a new beginning—a chance to clear one's mind, reconnect with a spouse or family members, or visit a part of the world they've never seen. In business or marketing terms, reinvention is known by another name: repositioning. Repositioning means updating or changing the marketing of a product. Credit card companies and mortgage companies are playing the start-over angle with extreme success. Many banks are offering secured cards that allow people with a negative credit history to have the same convenience as those with traditional credit cards. But the sell doesn't stop there. The people who obtain these cards feel that they are also rebuilding their past credit history—and getting a second chance.

Some recent TV shows—like *Extreme Makeover*, where a person gets free plastic surgery—are strong examples of how strong the Reinventing Hot Button is in our society. Many of the reality shows on TV are offshoots of the makeover shows. *Wife Swap* allows people to start over with new families. A Canadian TV show displaced two modern families into a pioneer setting where the couples had to reinvent themselves to face life the way the pioneers did, giving up the possessions and materialistic outlooks they possessed. The fascinating parts of

marketing insight   Chat rooms are one of the biggest attractions on the Internet and are the ultimate venue for the reinventor. People who have not met before get to choose their persona and act it out. They relieve themselves of personal baggage because nobody knows them except as blips on the computer. Users write their own profiles, proclaiming to the world what they do or don't like about themselves—and how they wish to be seen, not as they *are* seen. They can control what they say and do to an extent they may not have in real life. It is a chance for people to express themselves and create the first impression that they wish to convey. Online communities are a chance to be someone different, and judging by the number of people who participate in them it is an opportunity many consumers are flocking to take advantage of. Just look at the enrollment in online dating services.

these shows are the aftermaths. More often than not, the subjects really felt a positive transformation, not just because they had a new appearance but also because they incorporated new values into their lives.

An obvious place to see people's desire for reinvention is in the plastic surgery boom that has happened in recent years. According to the American Academy of Facial and Reconstructive Surgery, there was a 22 percent overall increase in plastic surgeries in 2004 over the previous year alone. Plastic surgery is not only for the rich anymore. Many people save up funds in the desire to become a new person, or a person who is looked at differently by his or her peers. Some people say they get LASIK eye surgery to get better vision and lead a life without glasses or contacts. The LASIK process brings about a rush for others, as they see it as a life-changing alteration—a way to reinvent themselves by seeing normally—without glasses.

Sometimes losing weight or getting into better physical shape is a symbol of starting over. Weight Watchers, personal trainers, and upscale health clubs know that a key part of the reinvention process is having salespeople who can also serve the dual purpose of providing a mental incentive for the transformation. Weight Watchers meetings feature fun and applause when a member gets on the scale and shows the other members how much weight he or she has lost. And the people who lose weight get something they very rarely get in the real world—applause for shedding pounds, and in some cases, changing their life.

makeovers promise a "new you"
So why is there such prevalent interest today in reinventing one's life? For the same reason that reality TV is so popular.

Many people are not satisfied with who they are and what they've done with their lives. Dissatisfaction with who people think they are, their role in life, or economic dissatisfaction forces people to take inventory of themselves. They want to fix what they perceive is holding them back.

life makeovers

Consumers will change their whole lives around by moving to new places, getting divorces, having affairs, or just trying on new lifestyles. Teenagers can go through constant makeovers until they find the one that fits them best. Marketers play to that by evolving their clothes lines, makeup products, and musical preferences. And teens have a great deal of money to spend on themselves.

Packaged Facts, a well-respected research company that tracks spending, asserts that:

- Family expenditures on teens will exceed $128 billion in 2006.
- Buying power of older teens will exceed $100 billion in 2006.
- Teen buying power will show an increase of 27.7 percent.

vision (as in values) makeover

A major group of reinventors are the baby boomers; they frequently undertake some dramatic life transformation. They want the freedom to remake themselves without the constant need of taking care of children. Many have gone as far as they can go in their lives and oftentimes their goals are unmet. Starting over gives them a new way to achieve their dream. For instance, they can move to a new place where no one knows them. They are not burdened by other people's preconceived notions about them.

attitude makeovers

This is the hardest type of makeover and the easiest for charlatans and cults as they try to provide a quick fix for attitudes that we may have been born with. Essentially, an attitude makeover is self-improvement for the mind. Marketers try to exploit this hot button with courses and Web sites like Beginner Triathlete.com (*www.beginnertriathlete.com*), whose blurb says "The journey begins in the brain. The brain, which energizes your attitude, is the most powerful factor in a lifestyle overhaul." Pretty heady stuff. Perhaps the first popular example of a makeover success was Dr. Norman Vincent's Peale's book *The Power of Positive Thinking*, which sold millions of copies.

Reinvention is everywhere you look in our society. Actors and actresses remake themselves constantly. Madonna has gone from self-proclaimed sex goddess to an author of children's books. Cosmetic companies have long embraced the desire to start over with products of all kinds that promise a chance to reinvent oneself with a new look or a chance to remove wrinkles and blemishes for a "new you." Even car companies allow customers to reinvent themselves every year by coming out with new models and product updates.

Rarely is a makeover or reinvention taken on overnight. It is more of an evolutionary process. That's why the marketer, as enabler, is so important. The marketer helps makeover candidates roll with the punches, adjust to the changing environment, and sustain, and even improve, on their conditions.

people don't grow up with the intention of reinventing

Statistics indicate that more than 75 percent of the population are unhappy with either their job, career, or family life. Many people don't have passion in what they are doing and feel truly unfulfilled. Too often, they selected their careers or made personal life choices when they were too young to really know what they wanted. Their choices were based on what they considered practical at the time, socially acceptable, or what they thought would bring them stability in the long run.

The problem is that many people find that the choices made at age twenty-five don't fulfill them when they are forty or fifty. Changing direction is risky, forbidden, or unknown; in many cases, personal or family obligations make life changes much too difficult. But a hot button marketer can get around this problem. A really good way to get around this is to minimize the risk of change. For instance a seller of a college program might state the following to get around fear:

Prospect: "I'm going to be too old in four years to make use of a college degree."

The hot button marketer's answer: "How old are you going to be if you don't take this course? This course may change your life or it may not. But one thing is for sure. You're going to be in the same place you are right now if you don't take this first step."

Successful hot button marketers eliminate the fear of starting over.

the joy of starting over

The world changes. The self-aware consumer feels that he or she must change to fit into the new order and to evolve with the new challenges. Products and sales approaches have to evolve, too. Products have to start over, as do companies. The chairman of Rubbermaid meets with each of Rubbermaid's business groups a couple of times annually to share ideas as well as to challenge them. In fact, their whole theme of business is based on reinvention, says the chairman: "People have the ability to reinvent themselves and open themselves up to the risk of change."

Whether people approach reinvention intentionally or just fall into it because of circumstance, starting over gives people a whole new outlook on life. As I was told in a marketing interview, "I began to change in a small way, by hiring a personal trainer. I began to realize I didn't have to look like my mother or share her values. Before that, I would never have had liposuction. My reinvention was part of self-discovery. I like my new look. I have a sense of reinventing myself."

Self-discovery is enhanced by and enhances reinvention. To reinvent oneself, the customer has to be:

- Open to reinvention
- Willing to try small steps until it becomes almost an obsession

The person, in the process of self-discovery, seeks ways of doing this. The marketer providing goods, services, and support is a conduit.

Many businesspeople say the best part of their life was building their business. They received a great deal more satisfaction in building than in sustaining their success. That's one of the reasons people switch careers or businesses in midstream.

The ways people try to start over include:

- Going back to school or learning a new trade
- Changing their hairstyle or wardrobe
- Taking a trip
- Kicking bad habits or trying to get rid of other imperfections
- Flirting with the opposite sex
- Quitting a job or entering a new field
- Joining an overseas volunteer organization
- Embracing a new religion
- Getting a divorce
- Moving to another state or country

Commitment refers to how important something is to the prospect and how determined he or she is to make a change happen. Look at the level of commitment the person has in changing him or herself. Empower them to fulfill that commitment. People make lifestyle changes for a variety of reasons. The hot button marketer helps them do so by empowering them—providing them with encouragement and inspiration to make the desired transformation.

pushing the hot button

for marketers
- Empower your customers to take the next step.
- Coach self-help methods effectively and supportively.

- Show testimonials, and before-and-after case histories or photos in your ads and brochures for whatever part of the makeover you're doing.
- Use a spokesperson who can become the "voice of your company." If that person has some ownership in the company, even better.
- Your program should create a variety of checkpoints, like losing a set amount of weight that will inspire customers.

for salespeople

- As mentioned in this chapter, you are both salesperson and empowerer. It's your job to keep the customer committed.
- Use store-bought inspirational material, like books, posters, and audio tapes, to keep uplifting the customer. Constantly reinforce goals.
- According to Steve Chandler and attorney Scott Richardson, in their book *100 Ways to Motivate Others*, a commitment to reinvention is an agreement with oneself to change one's life. Their advice? "Don't manage people, manage agreements."
- Have your customer start the process by filling out a questionnaire. One of the questions you can ask is "How would you like to change your life?" Read the answers closely before interviewing them. Use the "loaded" words at the beginning of this chapter as often as possible.

chapter 18

make me smarter

what marketers need to know

One of the best quotes I've ever read was in an advertisement
about twenty years ago: "Half of knowledge is knowing where
to find it." And finding it is one of the great enjoyments of life.
Better-informed consumers make more and better decisions.
Hot button marketers know how to make a customer feel smart
for buying a product or service. Hot button marketers also supply the information the prospect needs and wants. Knowledge
is an innate desire. People want to know more and learn more.
They want to feel they are smart and have other people recognize their intelligence. Knowledge is a key, if underused, part
of hot button marketing.

how marketers can apply this

Hot button marketers stimulate and challenge their consumers.
They make them want to learn more about their products and
services. Hot button marketers know how to make a customer
feel smart for buying a product. Hot button marketers also supply the information the prospect needs and wants, being careful to tailor that information to the consumer's level of interest
and need-to-know. They listen to their customers and try to fit
their products into what their customers want.

the knowledge conundrum

You're probably thinking, "This whole book is about emotion and the irrationality of the human purchase behavior and now we're talking about appeals to the intellect?"

In a word, yes.

People want to believe they are smart—and, they want others to think they're smart.

words to use in knowledge-based campaigns	
did you know?	where
how to	when
who	wow
what	why

The Make Me Smarter Hot Button is a highly underrated hot button, because until the beginning of the information age, we were in a sell-and-be-sold environment. The Internet has changed all that. Today we have access to more information at the touch of a key on a keyboard than in the history of humankind.

In addition to the Internet, consumers have a great many other ways to learn and arm themselves with information than they ever did before as a result of better education, as well as the proliferation of radio, TV, publishing venues, and other communications media. This accessibility to all kinds of information has changed the way consumers behave and expect to be treated in buy/sell scenarios. Moreover, the Make Me Smarter Hot Button is one that transcends all demographic groups.

what is the make me smarter hot button?

Why is there an insatiable quest for knowledge? Because being better informed helps consumers make better decisions about everything—from the products they buy to the life choices they make. Knowledge is about finding alternatives to "the ordinary." Being knowledgeable helps people function better in more complicated times. Knowledge fulfills the Discovery Hot Button as well. It fills in the blanks that people can't experience. You may not be able to afford to go to Paris, but you can buy a book on it.

In business, access to knowledge helps managers understand both their market and their employees. Said one manager, "If I understand where people are coming from, I can use their strengths, instead of being forced to deal with their weaknesses."

Knowledge can also be entertainment when it's knowledge that is accumulated without any expectation of having a use for it; for instance, watching a travelogue or a biography on TV. James Michener is a master of "knowledge as entertainment." He masterfully intertwines a plot into descriptions of lands and peoples. People are enthralled by the way Michener details his stories about places they might not have seen or heard about. Products are fun, but they come and go. Knowledge is fun *and* it can be with us forever.

Consider that Word Power has been a staple of *Reader's Digest* magazine for more than sixty years. Knowledge is power

marketing insight   Are libraries outdated? No way! According to a U.S. News/CNN Gallup poll, 67 percent of American adults visited a public library at least once in the past year. All of these visitors have, at some level, a desire to learn more about something. They need to attain some knowledge that will enable them to get more out of life. This is a very strong need.

both for the consumer and for the hot button marketers who sell to those who respond to the pull of knowledge. When the Rover landed on Mars, people were enthralled. Was it because humankind accomplished a great feat? Possibly, but if that were all, our interest would have been piqued only momentarily. But we wanted more. Was that a river we saw on the red planet or just a formation of rocks? We kept looking at photo after photo that the Lander sent our way. Why do we care what's beyond Saturn's rings? What's so important about Papua's dating rituals? These things don't affect us. Or, perhaps they do. The landing served as a stimulus to wanting to learn more. Knowledge in and of itself is its own stimuli, and for those who respond to the Make Me Smarter Hot Button, it can be highly addictive.

smartness is a state-of-mind, not a reflection of an iq test

People want to think they're smart. Hot button marketers play on this instinctual behavior. While it's expensive to educate consumers, it's a highly effective way to influence them. Smart hot button marketers use ads, packaging, brochures, Web sites, and telephone calls to inform and educate prospective customers. Look at all the ads for pharmaceuticals. People are greatly influenced by them. People will ask their doctors for prescriptions for a particular drug based on how they feel and how they succumb to the ads. The fact that the ads are working is proven by the proliferation of these ads. If drug companies thought they weren't working, they would stop the advertising. The trick is to let your customers know that they are as smart as you, but that you can execute the service better than anyone else—and perhaps add a bit of what they don't know.

For consumers affected by the Make Me Smarter Hot Button, acquiring knowledge goes way beyond researching a product to get a great deal or saving money on the purchase. The power for them is in learning something they didn't know before. The power is in learning something their neighbors, friends, and colleagues don't know. In some respects, learning about something can be a doorway into another peer group or social class.

The upshot is that marketers and salespeople can no longer simply present a product and hope to sell it. Consumers feel that the more they see, hear, and feel, the more they know. Consumers today engage in a much more proactive way of making decisions than marketers are used to. Car salespeople claim that, thanks to *Consumer Reports,* customers know even more about a particular car and its pricing than they do. Hot button marketers must go into the frame of reference of their prospects and assume they have done their research.

Today's consumers are more scrutinizing of major purchases and high-ticket items and services than they are for smaller, everyday purchases. For smaller purchases, consumers tend to get their knowledge more from the point of sale than from reading up on a product—although well-constructed and written hot button advertising can play a role. Better-educated

marketing insight   Curiosity may have killed the cat, but documentaries (in both audio, visual, and print format) and exposés do very well. They satisfy that innate need in humans to learn. Two of the hottest cable TV channels are the History Channel and the Discovery Channel. Two of the bestselling magazines are *National Geographic* and *Smithsonian* magazine. All of these are models of esoterica. Viewers and readers, for the most part, can't use the information in their own lives, but they get a kick out of learning what they never knew before.

consumers will rely on their own research, while lesser-educated consumers will filter this information as they gain input from peers. In fact, a finance company whose market was newly arrived Hispanics lessened their reliance on their translators, because they found that customers in search of knowledge were more receptive to information when it came from their own translators. The customers wanted the information they received about the products and services to be free from bias.

being smarter helps people get an edge

Chances are you bought this book to get an edge on the competition. Perhaps you wanted to get a better feel for your customers' desires and how you can build better relationships with them. As a marketer or salesperson you want to hit the hot buttons your competitors are missing. Knowledge brings a feeling of empowerment and enables consumers to make better buying decisions. However, with the proliferation of books and periodicals, a 24-7 news media, and the volume of information available via the Internet, customers can get lost or overwhelmed in their search for knowledge. Take advantage of it.

marketing insight   Blogs are journals written for the Internet. In theory they serve no purpose except as a means of publishing the writer's own thoughts and observations. However, blogs are increasingly being used to gather and search for information. Many bloggers write down their ideas and get feedback from readers. They feel that their knowledge is enriched by hearing other people's points of view and through exchanging thoughts and ideas.

You can search blogs and find out what the writers think of your product and get insights into what people are thinking and what they want. Send samples of your product to bloggers with heavy followings, and suggest that they mention your product if they like it. Yes, you really can blog your way to success.

Customers today have a wealth of information at their disposal; however, most people constantly complain they don't have enough time to read all the things they must. (Witness the declining subscriptions to newspapers.) Hot button marketers can handle this in different ways. Consider putting your message on a CD or cassette so that people can multitask—for instance, listen to it while they do their daily commute. Soundview Press publishes very short, pointed summaries of business books that contain new ideas, called "Executive Summaries." Speed-reading classes also impart ways to learn more in less time. Find ways to educate your customer while helping them sort through the plethora of information. If you do, your product or service will be differentiated from all the white noise.

the new consumers do everything they can to learn about the products they buy

Even the most mundane of products catch the consumer's intellectual (as well as emotional) attention. Watch a customer make a buying decision about a so-called parity product, like American cheese. Watch her pick up a product, then put it down. Watch her compare labels and prices. The ingredient label and nutrition facts have become her bible. Seafood departments and produce departments now have recipe books and preparation guides. They even offer computer terminals to show how to identify the best product in a given category. She will grill the people in the seafood department on how they handle their goods. She knows the difference between farm-raised salmon and fresh-caught salmon. The consumer is more knowledgeable than most marketers believe.

However, the fact that there is more information generally available about goods and services means that there is the potential for more misinformation to be available to your customer base. This misinformation can hurt your business. It's up to you, as a hot button marketer, to correct this by proactively making sure the information portrayed about your product or brand is accurate, even when the information does include a unique spin.

Many triggers apply to the need to know. Think of your product in terms of your prospect's curiosity and need to know. In the following exercise, check every option that your product can satisfy and fill in the blank with how your product satisfies that need.

	The entertainment factor	
	To make better choices	
	To improve one's life	
	To keep one's mind occupied	
	To learn something new	
	To keep one's mind sharp	
	To improve mental efficiency	
	To hope	
	To build self-confidence	
	To find out how to do something new	
	To discover alternate plans that can be followed when plan A doesn't work out	

A major clothing manufacturer, SYMS, created a hugely successful advertising campaign that said, "The Educated

Consumer Is Our Best Consumer." This simple campaign won a war of words with retailers who hyped their products as being the best. To consumers, merely saying they were the best didn't mean anything. Consumers want to know why. SYMS made a point of telling consumers why their products were better. They used the Make Me Smarter Hot Button very effectively—and debunked misinformation about their product.

build on your customer's quest for knowledge.

Your customer wants to feel smarter for using and choosing your product. As in the I'm Better Than You Hot Button (see Hot Button #2), she wants to show her intelligence off to her friends. You can make your consumer feel smarter by giving your product a new function that the other guy hasn't thought of yet. This makes consumers feel clever and like they're getting something for nothing. The value of your product is increased. Multipurpose cleaners make the consumer feel smarter by solving two problems at once.

real-life example   Hot button marketing has entered the health care industry. To many doctors' dismay, consumers are taking more control (see Hot Button #1) of their own health. Doctors and hospitals have traditionally received poor grades when it comes to educating their consumers. In many cases, doctors are actually taught that educating a patient reduces compliance and could make the patient more resistant to a prescribed course of treatment. Thus, many MDs may prescribe a pill or procedure and leave the consumer with a great many unanswered questions. So where does a patient find out about the side effects of a medication? From the hot button marketers at Walgreen's and CVS who take great pains to *ask* their customers if they have any questions about the medication they're purchasing. Patients feel in control by knowing what to expect and why their doctor prescribed it. A little knowledge can be very empowering.

Try making a minor cosmetic change to your product or service, but tie it into the consumer's knowledge base. Frank Perdue created a frenzy in the chicken business when he capitalized on the fact that his chickens had a brand name and yellow skin. This convinced consumers that Perdue chickens were healthier, premium chickens. They seemed healthier to consumers because Perdue positioned himself as an expert and he asserted that yellow was better. Consumers like to get their information from so-called experts, and Frank Perdue succeeded in positioning himself as one.

don't sell, inform

As mentioned in Chapter 8, sales trainer and executive Bud Holbert refuses to sell anything. He lets the consumer buy. He believes the days of selling are dead. "People are often too smart for that," he says. "They want the information they need to make the proper decision. I am merely an educator." In fact, he won't sell a prospect a product unless he's sure they have enough information to make a buying decision. Contrary to the way most non–hot button marketers work, he won't even close the deal the same day. He tells his prospects to wait until the next day, or until they have the information they need to make the proper decisions. He related a story about a customer to whom he refused to sell a policy. Why? She wouldn't weigh the pluses and minuses of the purchase.

Progressive Auto Insurance has played the "Inform, Don't Sell" strategy with amazing success. Their advertising says, "Go to our Web site and we'll show you the costs from the major insurance companies, so you can make an informed choice." They've taken an approach that used to be anathema to sales and marketing—giving the customer information about your competitor's products—and used it to their advantage.

Knowledge and the need to be smarter afford hot button marketers fertile ground for marketing strategies. Holiday Inn Express played on this hot button by creating an ingenious ad around it. The ad showed a person who was able to come up with a great idea. How? Because he'd just gotten a good night's sleep at the Holiday Inn Express. Of course, the ad was done in a tongue-in-cheek style, but it's a good example of Holiday Inn tapping the Make Me Smarter Hot Button in their customers. The idea, of course, is to use your imagination—get creative and get smart. It rubs off.

pushing the hot button

for marketers

- Position yourself or your company as an expert in the field in one facet or another. Hold seminars, write books, or get interviewed on TV or radio.
- Become a source of opinions and/or fact for trade magazines in your field. Develop an informative Web site.
- Educate your customers in every way possible, through infomercials, your packaging, your brochures, and seminars, etc.
- Tie your product into documentaries and other ways of getting education. Your customers will learn something, and the halo effect will reflect back into your company and product.
- Create educational newsletters, both in e-mail and print formats, to educate customers in a particular area of

interest. Be factual and helpful. Shell Oil created a series of brochures about how to keep cars running longer. American Express' Open for small businesses has expert advice on growing a business. Don't make these hard-sell pieces, because they will be seen as advertising.

for salespeople

- Educate your customers. Don't sell to them. If you sell against customers' perceived knowledge, you will always be in a defensive position,
- Ask questions to gauge the prospect's knowledge and build your pitch from there.
- Remind customers how intuitive or smart they are—but don't overdo it—or it comes off as being condescending and insincere.
- Don't contradict your customers, even if they're wrong. Restate their thoughts in a positive way. For instance, the customer says, "I've read that the Toyota Prius gets sixty-two miles per gallon." You say, "Sixty-two miles per gallon is technically feasible, but our customers are averaging forty-six miles per gallon and are very happy with it." You will be admired for your honesty.
- Prepare yourself with material and reviews from respected independent sources, even if they mention other brands.
- If you sell a service, like advertising, cite documented consumer trends and throw in some ideas.
- People love case histories. Cite them as often as possible.
- Position your pitch as "information gathering" rather than sales.

chapter 19

power, dominance, and influence

what marketers need to know

Hot button marketers know that the drive for power and influence affords them uncommon opportunities for working with some consumers. They instill their products and sales pitches with an aura of power that promises customers more dominance and influence. Consumers and leaders want power over external events, others, and themselves. In many ways, this is a restatement of the Control Hot Button.

how marketers can apply this

Provide something special for your customer that can increase their power or, at least, keep it. Why? Because when you have that special product or service, your customer doesn't just want you, they *need* you, to help keep the status quo. Your customers may want power, dominance, or influence. In America we hold whatever power we have dear and we don't want it robbed from us. Power is fine. It's desirable, even necessary. Influence over others is part of power. It's power's respectable cousin. The word *influence* connotes images of subtle persuasion and win-win situations.

However, we refuse to let ourselves be *dominated*, so we accept control. Power gets a bad rap. But it is an important hot button. So what is the Power Hot Button, and what is power itself?

Power is the capacity to influence others and their behavior. While the Control Hot Button is an insurance policy against negative things happening in our environment, the Power Hot Button is the ultimate mastery of our environment. Having power is not the same as using it. Even though the black belt karate master may be capable of exerting physical force over other people, the first thing karate academies teach is that although you can win the fight, it's best to walk away. There is power in walking away from an uncomfortable situation. There is little power in fighting back, unless it's necessary, because we lose power when we let someone else get under our skin. When you let emotions get to you, you lose.

the two kinds of power

Power is a broad hot button that applies to both individuals and to groups. We can go into a huge discourse about power, but for your purposes as a hot button marketer or salesperson, you need to know the two different types of power.

---

real-life example   I had the good fortune to be involved in the development of Smart Start Cereal for Kellogg's. As part of the project we developed concept boards that looked like real ads, and we showed them to groups of female consumers. One of the boards showed a woman in an office, dressed up in the latest power clothes and obviously supervising a group of people. Although we produced fifteen other boards, the women reacted strongest to the power concept. I asked them how they expected a cereal to generate "power" in them. They said that the cereal could give them energy to get through the day—enough energy to exert power. The imagery of the ad was what they aspired to. The advertising agency pounced on our lead and created an advertising campaign based on the theme *carpe diem*—"seize the day." It was a hard-hitting campaign about power.

1. **Personal power.** The consumer earns the right to wield influence over others by using his or her skills and talents.

2. **Positional power.** A person has dominance because of a ranking or job. Kings, matriarchs, or people who are accorded a position of power by virtue of their birth are acceptable role definitions for positional power. You might also think of an umpire at a baseball game having strong positional power. In a family, power can be the influence you have over your children's behavior.

To be fair and thorough, we can accurately say that everyone has the power and ability to influence others almost every day in some aspect of his or her life. They will also guard it zealously, whether it's the parent, or the child who throws a temper tantrum in a quiet restaurant to exert influence over his parents.

symbols of power

As was previously mentioned, symbols are shortcuts. They bypass conscious consideration, triggering deeply embedded subconscious responses. For example, when you see a person in a luxury car, a wide range of associations about them may immediately spring to mind, often accompanied by various feelings and emotional reactions such as admiration, jealousy, or inferiority. This is the heart and soul of what the power-oriented consumer wants.

The purpose of many symbols is to communicate power. We are programmed to conform with many symbols, such as a policeman's uniform or the elegant Rolex watch studded with diamonds on the prospect's wrist. These types of symbols are not always there for show or to show off prestige, but to communicate power, influence, and strength.

Power ties, Mont Blanc Pens, and the Black American Express card—these are all products that reflect social dominance. They reek of affluence and influence. Most people don't know about the Black American Express Card, or the Centurion Card. American Express issues a special black card that allows its holders to buy anything. Consumers can't even apply for the card. They have to be invited. Using it for lunch with a client is the ultimate power trip.

Wealth is frequently equated with power and in some ways it is power. Wealth enables consumers to buy whatever they want and to exert influence over others. Knowledge is power because it can make individuals vital to their peer groups or companies. For example, suppose you're the only one who knows the recipe for that secret sauce.

While power is thought of as a whole lifestyle situation, people can possess power in different ways. An administrator with limited power in a corporation may be the head of a building committee at home. A schoolteacher may head up a local charitable organization. Almost everyone has power on his or her home turf, whatever that might be. And, of course, the epitome of power is the secretary of the buyer you are trying to get to. All have to be approached differently, especially in the corporate world.

selling to middle management

This is the area where most hot button salespeople get bogged down. For the most part middle managers are just screeners.

They have little or no decision-making powers. They have to sell to upper management. Usually they will say, "It sounds interesting. Let me tell my boss." Don't let this happen. Offer to make your pitch to the boss directly. No one will be as persuasive as you are. Middle managers, by the nature of their position, must kowtow to upper management, which has the real power (not counting stockholders).

In middle management, you sell by what's in it for the middle manager (and secondarily) the company. It could be a promotion, more money, or an "in" to more power. It's up to the hot button marketer to make middle managers look good.

how do you get to upper management?

Usually, when you visit a client, you will be asked if you'd like some coffee or tea. Accept graciously. Your very sales success may depend on it. Why? Because the act of accepting your client's hospitality acknowledges that, in the scheme of things, he is above you. You're allowing him or her to feel both powerful and in control.

Thankfully, due to the reform of the company caste system, most secretaries are not expected to deliver coffee. It's not uncommon for you to accompany a middle manager to the coffee machine. That's a good thing. At the coffee machine everybody is equal. The middle manager is at ease here and frequently is comfortable enough to answer most informal discussions, like "Who is going to make the ultimate decision?" You will often get the right name. At this time—or at another casual moment—say the following: "You know, statistics say 90 percent of the information is lost when you pass it on to a fellow worker. May I present this to him personally? I'd like you to be there, of course." Remember, middle management is the screener. If you came across well at this point, you will be given the opportunity to make your presentation to the decision-maker.

selling to the power brokers

While middle managers want to know what's in it for themselves, upper management wants to know what's in it for the company. Upper managers are particularly concerned about what's in it for the company because that's where they get their power. Upper managers have already proven themselves and secured their positions, at least to the powers that be. They have spent their time demonstrating their talents, education, and ability. Now they want to show off their power. They are the typical "Power-Centered Consumer" you are trying to sell to.

One of the common denominators of the power-oriented customer is that he or she is always reading you. Learning about people is one of the ways that they build networks and influence others. They have to be able to cajole, influence, and occasionally manipulate in order to get what they want out of subordinates, partners, and investors alike. In any selling situation, the key players focus on sizing up each other. Each is trying to exert influence over the other. The smart hot button marketer understands the prospect's power and understands that in the mind of the power buyer, the salesperson is an adversary.

That doesn't mean that you, as a hot button marketer, are without power. You have something the buyer can use to look, feel, or become even more powerful. What are your bargaining chips? Material goods that will make the individual look even more powerful? Information or sources of information that the prospect can't get anywhere else? A unique service that reaffirms their power status? Cater to the powerful consumer to maintain the status quo.

what do people in power positions usually buy?

It depends on how assertive the power-oriented buyer wants to be. People in a position of power usually buy what they consider is best for the company and its employees because the decisions reflect on the company, not the person. The person is often self-assured so he doesn't need the physical "showoff perks" of dominance or influence.

Sam Walton, founder of Wal*Mart, drove an old pickup truck until he died. Many other people, however, try to exert power with luxury cars. This is similar to those who respond to the I'm Better Than You Hot Button. The difference is their goal is to show off their power and influence—not their status.

Mark McCormack, author of *What They Don't Teach You at Harvard Business School: Notes from a Street-Smart Executive*, talks about going to lunch with the managing editor of *Time* magazine. When they reached the restaurant, the *Time* magazine manager greeted the maitre d' of a restaurant that catered to the rich and powerful with "Good to see you again." Nothing wrong with that, you might say, but the managing editor had never met the maitre d' before. It was a pretense. He was making a point of showing off his influence with the movers and shakers.

You should be real when trying to sell to leadership. Smart leaders can see right through the haze you build around yourself. When making impressions, be subtle. Be aware of the image and sales flow you are trying to create. Oftentimes, arriving in a limo, ordering the finest champagne, or dressing to the max creates a false impression, and you're the fall guy. Earlier in this book we spoke about dressing better than the client. Power dressing is the right of the person who holds the dominant position. He doesn't want you to dress better than him. When selling to power brokers dress conservatively so that your emotions can't be read.

tips for selling to power-oriented prospects

Sell to their strengths, not their weaknesses. Power-oriented prospects filter out their own weaknesses. In fact, a power-oriented leader is sometimes put off by an emotional selling strategy that would move other consumers. He has been taught, or learned, not to show emotions so others can't read his strategies or intentions.

Understand where you can act proactively and where you can only react—or perhaps choose not to react at all. Let the leaders ask the questions, as if the products were coming from them; then, make deliberate choices as to what power you will use or not use, and in what way. Remember, the reason he or she will buy your product will be to reinforce his or her leadership positioning.

As you may have heard, you're never a hero in your own home. So when corporate executives don their dark pinstriped suits, they will act the part. Remember, though, that this may be a far cry from the way they are at home where frequently the cry from their spouses or children will be "get into some shorts; you have to take out the garbage." Thus, how you sell to a power broker may change with the venue or situation. They may hold positional power at the office but not necessarily when they are shopping for a new sofa with their spouse.

Some requisites for selling to the power-oriented consumer or corporate buyer:

1. **Alphas (the dominant ones) need to know your purpose.** Power-oriented consumers design their lives and their symbols around a leadership purpose. They have a clear vision of what that purpose is and how the marketer can help with that purpose.

2. **Commit to the leader's corporate goals.** With a clear vision and purpose, power-oriented consumers establish the road map to be used when establishing their reputation. They want you to be as committed as they are.

3. **Reputation is key.** Their reputation is one of their most valuable assets. Sell to the reputation. Understand how the reputation was built and how it is best maintained or enhanced.

4. **Make suggestions and be a consultant.** Open-minded, power-oriented prospects know that they don't have all the answers. They know that to have sustained success they have to be open to all possibilities.

5. **Offer them continuous improvement/innovation.** Power-oriented consumers are in a never-ending cycle of improving themselves and whatever they touch. They read the latest material in their field of study. They expand their territory and seek innovative ways to expand their horizons.

6. **Be decisive.** They use you as a resource and your role is to enable them to be confident that they're making the best decision.

When using this hot button, or selling to dominant and influential prospects, show them something that can increase their power and dominance. Middle managers tend to buy things that can increase their personal dominance and may help them look good to higher-ups. Upper management usually wants products that are good for the company, because, in their minds, they are the company—and it helps reinforce their position. But, even outside the corporate setting, almost everyone has moments of power and dominance. It's up to the hot button marketer to cater to these people—and these moments. We all want to be looked up to. That's what power and dominance is all about. Reinforce the prospect's feelings and you have a winning selling proposition.

pushing the hot button

for marketers

- Use giveaways and large marketing thrusts to show that you will be dominant and stay dominant. This will help you build momentum.
- Run commercials in high-profile media. Stay high profile with a constant flow of press releases highlighting your innovative breakthroughs.
- Build quantitative measurements into everything you do, so both middle management and leaders can track and see progress.
- Sell the benefits of your program or product, rather than the features.

- Create products and services that will make dominants "stars" within their company. Stress how your product can favorably position your client to others.

for salespeople

- Understand who's in charge and makes the final buying decision. It may take four or five presentations until the truth comes out or until you reach the entire chain of command. Find out all you can about the sign-offs needed to close the sale.
- Make your presentations as often as you have to. Don't rely on others to make your sale for you. Learn the background of the decision-makers, including their work style. You can usually get that from their underlings.
- Show attention to detail and be methodical in your arrangement of facts and numbers. Show comparisons with similar products or services. Don't go crazy with testimonials, because the dominant customers tend to ignore them—only his or her opinion counts.
- Play up the person's ego in everything you say and do. Try to get an impressive sounding title on your business card. This is especially important in cross-cultural marketing.

chapter 20

wish fulfillment

what marketers need to know

People covet many things. Many of people's emotional yearnings have been distilled in this book—the need for control and the desire for family values, as well as adventure and prestige.

Each hot button speaks to certain consumers who have these specific burning desires that need to be filled. They represent the primary dreams and wishes that motivate consumers—the home in the mountains, the finest cars, kids that kiss and hug Mom and Dad when they come home from work. These are all aspirations. Hot button marketers look for what a consumer's deepest dreams are and then find ways to give them power to fly.

how marketers can apply this

There are many situations where you might want to use a "wish list" with your prospect or customer. The best method is to have the prospect fill in the blank to the following statement: "I'm glad George (or whatever your name is) came here because _____." Customers will often tell you their wishes if you prompt them. (See Chapter 4 for more suggestions on how to prompt your customers.)

There are two keys for applying the hot button strategy to your customer's wish list.

- Find out what your prospects want and how to fit that into their dreams.
- Help them get what's attainable.

Let's say a prospect wants a new Lexus but obviously can't afford it. Sell the car that he or she *can* afford. You can use any number of different slants. You can, for example, say, "Well, we don't have a Lexus that you can afford, but you can have the next best thing. A new (or used) Toyota Camry. It's got the same roominess and quietness and an equivalent engine. No, it's not a Lexus, but when you're ready to trade it in, your finances may have changed. Then, you can trade in your Camry for an affordable Lexus." It's important to let your customers know that the product will help them attain some portion of their wish list and that their main wish will be attainable.

let's talk about wish fulfillment

According to the dictionary, wish fulfillment is the gratification or satisfaction of a desire, need, or impulse through a dream, fantasy, or other exercise of the imagination. Yes, wish fulfillment is a product of our imagination.

In reality, the handsome lover may be a slob who leaves his socks on the floor. Immortality may be the Greek myth where two lovers were offered a chance to be ageless but they were turned into undying trees. And the dream of love may lead as much to heartache and tears as it does to bliss. However, hot button marketers understand that their job is to sell the dream as the consumer wants it. Sometimes that means selling a product or service that allows consumers to merely approach their aspirations even though we know that the product may fall short of the perfection of their dream. Wish fulfillment is symbolic. Yes, some dreams do happen. But they always come with a price to pay. The American Dream of a home in the suburbs with a white picket fence comes with a mighty mortgage.

Wishful thinking longs for everything to be perfect. But perfection is not reality. Hot button marketers understand that. They know that their products probably won't make the wish reality. But they do strive to come close. No, we can't all be famous baseball players, but for $3,200 we can go to baseball camps, and learn, play, and dine with our favorite baseball players. No, we can't all be like Steven Spielberg, but we can buy our own movie-making software and try to make movies like him. No, we can't be like the Brady Bunch but we can all attempt to instill feelings of togetherness in our families. No, we can't be immortal, but we can write journals and books that keep memories alive.

These are just a few of the ways we strive to fulfill our wishes. We want our wishes fulfilled—never mind if it's winning the lottery, a lifetime relationship with a particular person, or whatever else. Most of us don't get a shot at our real dreams, so we accept substitutes, putting what we really want in the back of our minds. Hot button marketers can at least partially help consumers pull out those hopes and dreams, dust them off, and encourage us to seek some level of wish fulfillment.

Lottery owners push the dream of wish fulfillment to the max. They rarely talk about the money going to education. Of course, considering the odds of winning the big prize are something like 170 million to one, chances are we are not going to win it anyway. So planning the next step is pretty much inconsequential. Nevertheless marketers play up the dream of winning "the big one" by offering mini-prizes: $5 to $20 prizes that reinforce the dream. These small prizes are just carrots. They keep people in the game. After all, if we can win the little one, why can't we win the big one? Casinos make money on the slots by selling dreams, too. We hear the bells and clacks go on incessantly, so we can hear how much everyone (we think) is winning. Casinos are all about wish fulfillment. One of the hotter TV show concepts is poker. We watch as a celebrity draws a winning card to an inside straight and we feel that we can do it, too.

how networking companies sell the dream

Most multilevel companies work the same way. They have their greatest success in tough economic times.

One multilevel company (the word used often today is *networking* company) sells telephone cards and services. New members get so involved in this life-changing activity that they don't realize that their potential clients can get cheaper services elsewhere. They get so carried away by the wish to be independent that they don't realize that they have to work as hard as if it were a full-time business.

Here's how a typical multilevel/network marketing pitch goes. You're invited to a meeting to look at a business. You rarely—if ever—know what the business or the product is until you get to the meeting. The meeting is held in a room packed with people (and usually you're charged a fee to participate). It's a celebratorial experience all the way. One speaker after another tells how she moved out of a tiny house. Creditors were knocking on her door. Both she and her husband lost their jobs. But they found a miracle with this particular product. Now their children are A-students in college, and they live in a mansion with sixteen butlers and a three-car garage for their Lexus, Mercedes, and Rolls. They now have more time to spend with their kids. People scream and cheer. Sometimes people cry at the opportunity they think they are getting.

If this sounds like a religious revival meeting, you're right. Very rarely are we able to confront our wishes and find a way to get them.

All the major networking companies sell inspirational tapes to keep customers' spirits high. There is a good reason for that. In fact, you can watch the impact of positive messages in the media on sales. When the news is negative or depressing, the stock market, and sales in general, waver. Consumers reason: "Why bother? I've got to attend to the business of survival." There's no room for fun, goal achievement, or dreams now. But whenever there's good news, especially news that implies that everything is looking up, retail sales skyrocket. Consumers reason: "*Now* is the time I'll be able to reach my dream."

Savvy hot button marketers cater to this hope. They understand that wish fulfillment is a product of suggestibility. They look for ways to remind consumers of their dreams, reaffirm the possibilities of achieving those dreams by using reinforcing suggestions, and then present solutions and paths that lead to fulfillment of consumers' wishes.

Suggestibility is best exemplified by the placebo response in the medical industry. Medical researchers and pharmaceutical companies will often compare new drugs against a placebo, which is oftentimes a sugar pill that has absolutely no medicinal properties. However, those placebos frequently yield unexpected results. Patients will often experience diminished symptoms as a result of placebos. Some have suggested that placebos work because we wish and expect the pain to go away, and so it does. Science has even shown that, while the placebo response is variable, its effectiveness has significantly increased in the past years. Scientists have posited that this phenomenon has something to do with endorphin levels. Be that as it may, placebos work best when combined with suggestions that reinforce what the placebo is supposed to do.

A hot button marketer also uses the placebo effect—suggesting that buying a product, like a lottery ticket, car, or even a massage, will cure all that ails them. The advertising industry exploits wish fulfillment by suggesting an association of their product with a specific desire (e.g., good health, attractiveness, or power). The agencies and their clients successfully spend billions of dollars every year because of our suggestibility.

what's at the top of the wish list?

Research finds that wishes know no demographic boundary. The president of a company may wish for a small job where he or she is not under pressure. A janitor may have the wish to own the company he's cleaning. Some wishes are easily attainable without much effort. Some are not. It depends on the caliber of the wish.

Laura King, Ph.D., of Southern Methodist University asked 405 college students what their top wish was. Just as in the old movies, they were given three wishes. While some of the wishes were outlandish and impractical, King did find many similarities—so marketers should take heed.

The most common wishes were for friends, happiness, health, marriage, money, success, self-improvement, and to help other people. More men than women wanted sex and power. More women wanted happiness, a better appearance, and greater health. Extroverts frequently wished to be happy and have positive feelings. They also frequently included other people in their wishes. Introverts, on the other hand, wished to be more sociable and more emotionally stable. Those who were already satisfied with their lives were the most likely to believe that their wishes would come true.

So while the wishes were consistent, it's most important to note that the specific top three desires varied depending on the personality type of the respondent. This is why it's critical to learn about your customer using the methods outlined in Chapter 4.

pushing the hot button

for marketers
- The wish varies with the wisher. For some it can be a beautiful set of teeth; for some it could be for more leisure time. Discover what a core, target group of consumers want, and make it for them.
- Mention the words "your dream" in your marketing. Let the customer fill in the blanks.
- Sell only the pleasant parts. It makes your customers feel better to pay attention to things they desire rather than to spend time thinking about less pleasant things.

for salespeople

- Use computer renderings to show the dream realized—what would your customer look like with that new hairstyle, or what would their house look like with a new addition.
- Sell the results of the dream, not the dream itself.
- Interview consumers to find out their greatest longing.
- Sell only the positive aspects of the dream. For instance, if the dream is a vacation in Acapulco, don't sell the fact that it's expensive.

a very brief conclusion

Sell the dream, not the reality. As marketers you have the power to give someone satisfaction that they can't achieve anywhere else. At least one of the hot buttons will apply to each of your prospects. We have been evolving for thousands (maybe millions) of years. Some of the hot buttons, like status, nurturing, and dominance, are primal and are shared with our cousins in the animal world. Some hot buttons are distinctly human, such as control and self-achievement.

Due to evolution and our planet's considerable resources, most of our physical needs are met, but not our psychological needs. As humans, our minds and emotions are the most difficult to discern. Like a fingerprint, everyone's mind and motivations are distinct. The hot button marketer gets past human facades and breaks these down to psychological wants and needs. You may not agree with these needs, but to be successful, you need to sell to them. Use this book as a guide to human motivations. Happy marketing.

a note from the author

Thank you for reading this book. If you have any ideas for future editions, or if you have a particular, or unusual, Hot Button strategy that worked for you, please contact me at:

Barry Feig's Center for Product Success
2 Camino Montoso
Santa Fe, NM 87508

My e-mail is *feig@barryfeig.com.*

index

about the author

BARRY FEIG is a leading consumer behaviorist. He has over two decades of experience developing new products and marketing strategies for companies such as American Express, Colgate-Palmolive, and First Brands. The products and strategies he has created have generated sales in excess of $3 billion and include such familiar products as Glad-Lock Storage Bags, Kellogg's Smart Start Cereal, American Express' Gift Cheques, and Ralston-Purina's Kibbles & Chunks. Prior to founding the Center for Product Success, Mr. Feig owned two New York advertising agencies, Ad Ventures and Feig Communications. His clients included IBM, Schenley Distillers, and Curtis Instruments. Mr. Feig has authored more than 100 articles for such publications as *Advertising Age* and *American Demographics*.